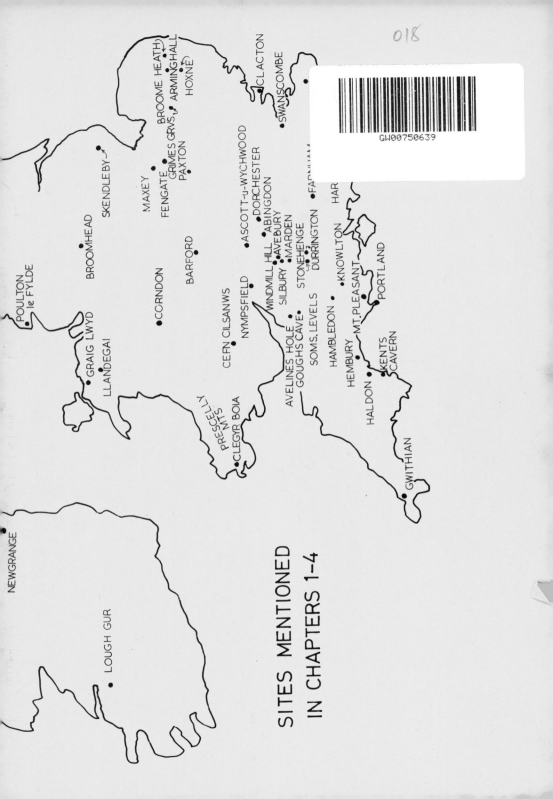

SITES MENTIONED IN CHAPTERS 1-4

018

GW00750639

NEWGRANGE

LOUGH GUR

POULTON le FYLDE

GRAIG LWYD

LLANDEGAI

BROOMHEAD

SKENDLEBY

MAXEY

FENGATE

GRIMES GRVS.

BROOME HEATH

ARMINGHALL

HOXNE?

PAXTON

CLACTON

SWANSCOMBE

CCRNDON

BARFORD

CEFN CILSANWS

NYMPSFIELD

ASCOTT-u-WYCHWOOD

DORCHESTER

ABINGDON

WINDMILL HILL

AVEBURY

SILBURY

MARDEN

STONEHENGE

DURRINGTON

FARNHAM

HAR

PRESCELLY MTS

CLEGYR BOIA

AVELINES HOLE

GOUGHS CAVE

SOMS. LEVELS

HAMBLEDON

KNOWLTON

MT. PLEASANT

PORTLAND

HEMBURY

HALDON

KENTS CAVERN

GWITHIAN

PREHISTORIC BRITAIN

An 'Acheulian' hand-axe of c.200,000 BC.

KEITH BRANIGAN

Prehistoric Britain

AN ILLUSTRATED SURVEY

SPURBOOKS LIMITED

PUBLISHED BY
SPURBOOKS LTD
6 PARADE COURT
BOURNE END
BUCKINGHAMSHIRE

ISBN   0 904978 01 X

Designed and produced by
Mechanick Exercises, London

Typesetting by Inforum Ltd, Portsmouth.
Printed in Great Britain by Redwood Burn Ltd,
Trowbridge and Esher.

TO TANIA

CONTENTS

ILLUSTRATIONS

9

The evidence for the elk-hunt described on pages 22-23 has now been questioned; see Proc. Prehist. Soc. 41(1975) 15-16.

PREFACE

Our understanding of the past is changing just as constantly and extensively as is our understanding of the present. All periods and areas of archaeological study have seen major changes of interpretation and emphasis in recent years, partly due to the ever-increasing amount of information and material available, partly due to new techniques of dating, analysis, and excavation, but above all because a new generation of archaeologists is looking at the evidence in a different way and through different eyes.

It has long been apparent to both students and teachers that a general, up-to-date survey of the history of Britain up to the time of the Roman conquest was needed, and this book is an attempt to provide such a survey. It is not intended as a text-book for the student but rather as a framework into which he or she can fit their more detailed studies, and from which the general reader can obtain an idea of how human society developed in these islands up until the time when it was dragged by conquerors into the realms of written history.

Readers will look in vain for those familiar terms which normally punctuate books on prehistory—Neolithis, Bronze Age, Iron Age and so on. These terms, though they may be little more than terms of convenience these days, nevertheless carry with them a suggestion that the important events in British (and other) prehistory were all technological ones. Few archaeologists would today support such a view and I have attempted to break away from the shackles imposed by these terms. Prehistory, which has to be written from the wordless and anonymous evidence of archaeology, is even more concerned with processes than is History, and for this reason it is difficult to divide it up into meaningful periods in the same way as we do History. Nevertheless this is what I have attempted to do, identifying eight major phases in the history of Britain prior to the Roman invasion.

The dates ascribed to these periods are, of course, approximate and all the more so the further back one goes in time. With the exception of some dates quoted in the last two chapters they are all based on carbon 14 dating. As many readers will know there are doubts about the accuracy of this method of dating, and in particular there are many who believe that many of the dates in the period c.8000 BC to 1500 BC are substantially too low or too young. At present it seems to me that the evidence favours C.14 dates calculated on what is known as the improved half-life of 5730 years, and dates quoted here are calculated on that basis.

In order to keep the text as readable and immediate as possible I have refrained from mentioning by name any of the dozens of archaeologists who by their studies and published work have contributed to the knowledge brought together and considered in this book. Some are mentioned in the suggestions for further reading but many must of necessity go unmentioned. I should like to acknowledge here the work of all British prehistorians, professional and part-time, who have together helped to 'write' this book. More particularly I must thank all those good friends and colleagues who have allowed me to reproduce photographs and who are mentioned by name in the list of illustrations. I must especially thank Gordon Kelsey who reproduced many photographs as well as taking others for this book in the City Museum, Bristol. I am very grateful to the staff there, and the director Mr. Nicholas Thomas, for so willingly allowing me to take several photographs in the galleries. Finally I must again record the interest and the help of my family—Nong, Alun and Holly—who have not only encouraged me to write the book but have walked many muddy fields in England, Scotland and Wales to allow me to gather illustrations for it.

CHAPTER ONE

250,000–4,000 BC

For Geoffrey of Monmouth, writing in the twelfth century AD, the history of Britain began in 1170 BC, when Brutus, a royal prince of Troy, landed at Totnes. Today we recognise that the beginnings of British history were far less dramatic and far more remote than this, so remote in fact that it is difficult for us to say very much about them with any certainty. The first inhabitants of these islands were probably only temporary visitors and may have reached here in one of the warmer episodes of the Anglian glaciation. This would have been sometime between 300,000 and 250,000 BC, not very long after the great ice sheet had reached its furthest point south and penetrated the Thames Valley. The only monuments to these early explorers are a few coarsely-worked and rather thick flint hand-axes, which, nevertheless, are widely distributed in Southern England, from Fordwich in Kent and Warren Hill in Suffolk, to Kent's Cavern near Torquay.

While the ice sheet persisted, however, conditions in Britain were not likely to attract a permanent population. It was only when the ice retreated and a prolonged 'interglacial' period of warmer weather began that small bands of hunters might find it worthwhile to occupy the southern regions of the country. Such a period began about 250,000 BC and lasted for perhaps 50,000 years. Temperatures rose, temperate forest spread, and the animal population changed as reindeer, horse, bison and mammoth were replaced by species who favoured the new woodland environment — straight-tusked elephant, deer, ox and boar. These changing conditions favoured man and he came to Britain with increasing frequency and in greater numbers. Initially, the hunters seem to have restricted their activities to the South-East corner of Britain, where a handful of sites, of which Clacton-on-Sea is the best known, has produced the heavy flakes of flint and the nodules and cores from which the flakes were struck, which formed the basic tool kit of these people. They also used wooden spears, from one of which a tip has miraculously survived, and no doubt utilised heavy sticks as clubs, and stones as medium-range weapons in their quest for food. One implement which was missing from their tool-kit, however, was the handaxe.

In this they differed significantly from the far more numerous hunters who arrived in Britain a little later and spread far more widely in the south of the country. These people, who for the sake of convenience we call 'Acheulians' after a site in France where their characteristic handaxes were found in large numbers, are represented at over three thousand places in Southern England. We have to remember of course that many axes represent accidental losses during hunting expeditions, and that we are dealing with axes made and lost over tens of thousands of years. Nevertheless, the population of Britain must have been much greater during the Acheulian period, than at any time prior to their arrival, and was probably not matched again until after the last of the Ice Ages had ended, about 8500 BC.

Most of the places where Acheulian hand-axes have been found are in river valleys, particularly those of the Thames and the Medway, and others were originally beside lakes. No doubt such locations not only ensured a supply of fresh water but were also good places in which to find and kill food animals. The Acheulians could not afford to settle in any one place, however, if they were to catch enough food to keep themselves through the year. Sites were occupied only for a short period, and they have left little evidence for the archaeologist to recover. At Stoke Newington in North London, however, a temporary camp site produced the remains of dumps of ferns which had possibly been used as beds, and two pointed, four-feet long, birch poles which may have formed part of a shelter. Elsewhere, occupation is usually represented only by a roughly cleared piece of ground on which the accumulated debris from making flint implements has collected. The importance of flint to the Acheulians is difficult to over-estimate, and is emphasised by the distribution of Acheulian sites in Britain. Only about three hundred sites out of a total of over three thousand are found north and west of a line drawn between the Bristol Channel and the Wash. It is precisely south and east of this line that flint of good quality is most readily available. The axes which were manufactured from the flint are very similar throughout not only Britain but much of Western Europe and they tell us a little about man's mental as well as his technical progress. The maker of an Acheulian hand-axe must have had a clear idea, at the outset of his work, of the finished product which he desired, and also of the sequence of blows which would produce that form. He was, quite certainly, mentally more advanced than earlier men, and his skeletal remains show that he possessed a larger brain. They also show that he possessed a smaller and shorter lower jaw, and that there were changes in the position of both the tongue and the larynx. Together with his mental progress, these changes are thought by some specialists to indicate that Acheulian man could combine syllables to make words. This would have allowed him to develop a much enlarged vocabulary, and therefore to communicate more efficiently with his fellows.

About 200,000 BC increasingly cold conditions forced the Acheulians to retreat from their hunting grounds in Britain and the ice, once more, advanced southwards. The climatic and other environmental changes which took place were not abrupt, of course, but occurred over a long period of time. These gradual changes are indicated by the increasing number of silver fir trees in the forests and by the re-appearance of essentially open-country animals like the horse amongst the food remains of late Acheulian hunters at sites such as Hoxne (Suffolk) and Swanscombe (Kent). From about 200,000 BC until about 25,000 BC, human occupation of Britain was sparse and irregular. Acheulian hunters, using a new method of producing ready-to-use implements by striking flakes from a carefully prepared core of flint, apparently sought their prey in the extreme south-east corner of England during some of the warmer ("interstadial") episodes of the third glaciation, and similar tools occur in the same area in the following interglacial period between 125,000 and 70,000 BC. But for some reason which is not yet apparent, the return of warmer conditions and the retreat of the ice did not bring the hunters back to Britain in anything like the same numbers as previously. What hunters there were may have specialised in mammoth hunting, and at Ealing one of the typical flake tools was found with the skeleton of a mammoth, probably indicating the spot where it had been attacked and killed by a small group of these men.

The last ice age, which began about 70,000 BC, was not as severe and extensive as earlier ones, the ice sheet reaching only as far south as York except in the west where it penetrated as far south as Central Wales. During its warmer episodes when temperatures may have been almost the same as those of the present day, the areas of grassland probably expanded at the expense of the tundra and mammoths, horse, bison and reindeer would have been sufficiently prolific to encourage hunters to occupy Southern England. At the same time the locking-up of so much water in the ice sheet meant that the sea level may have dropped by as much as a hundred metres and that Britain was part of the European mainland. The hunters who came to Britain during the first half of this last glaciation were of the physical type which has been known for so long as Neanderthal man. These were short, stocky men with a slouching carriage; their faces were dominated by a broad nose and protruding brows, above which the forehead receded sharply. Their hand-axes and other tools — points, scrapers and knives — are found widely but thinly scattered in Britain, as far north as Derbyshire and as far west as Denbighshire. Most of these temporary occupation sites which have been examined by archaeologists are not open sites like those occupied by earlier hunters in Britain, but caves and rock-shelters. It may be that Neanderthal man preferred his occupation sites to be a little less temporary and a little more secure than those who had preceded him, and that his hunting techniques had become sufficiently sophisticated to allow him to achieve this end. On the whole, however, it is more likely that these cave sites simply reflect his greater penetration of the upland areas where caves were to be found more easily. In one respect Neanderthal man does seem to differ significantly from his predecessors, and that is in his spiritual awareness. At present we have no evidence of this from Britain, but elsewhere Neanderthal man is known to have deliberately buried his dead, and to have done so with a certain amount of ritual. Although we still do not understand the relationship, if any, between Neanderthal man and those who succeeded him in southern Britain, it is interesting to note that the last of the Old Stone Age hunters also occupy caves, bury their dead, and reveal signs of spirituality.

These developments occur during the last twenty thousand years of the final Ice Age, between 30,000 and 8,500 BC, when two warm periods saw the arrival of further hunters. In the earlier of these two episodes cave sites in western Britain again produced most evidence of occupation, and in particular a series of long leaf-shaped flint blades which were probably used as spearheads. There are no signs in any of these caves, however, of even the most rudimentary 'cave art',

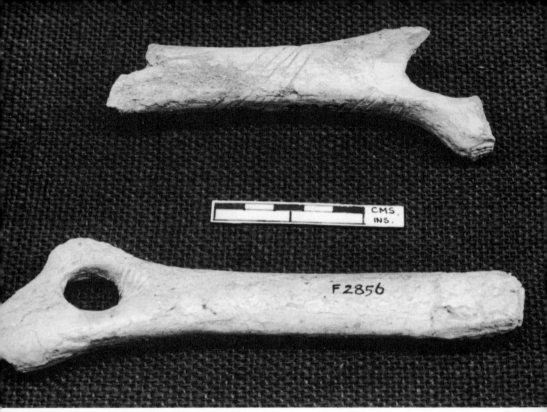

Bone 'batons' from Gough's Cave, Cheddar.

although their occupation is partly contemporary with the superb paintings which decorate caves in Southern France and Spain.

In the second warm period, on the other hand, there is a little more evidence for the practice of ritual, although its validity and significance is hard to assess. The caves of Mendip have produced several pieces of worked bone to which a ritual function might be ascribed of which two 'batons' found in Gough's Cave are the most notable. Each has a large perforation at one end of a smoothed shaft, and one example was possibly associated with a human burial dated (by C.14) about 9000 BC. Another, decorated, piece of rib bone carried a net-like design on one side and a series of short strokes, arranged in groups, on the other. It is comparable with more elaborately decorated bone artifacts found elsewhere in western Europe, and is most likely to be a tally of some sort.

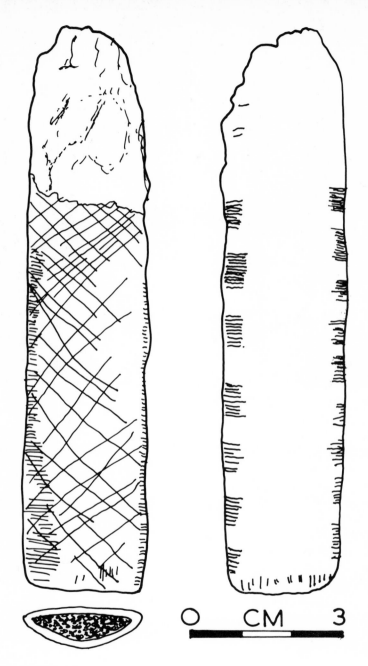

A decorated rib bone from Gough's Cave, Cheddar.

Aveline's Hole, Soms, used for burials c.12,000-9,000 BC.

Apart from the burial in Gough's Cave other burials of this period have been found in Mendip caves, notably in Aveline's Hole where several burials are attested. Two of these were found apparently associated with flint implements, worked animal teeth, and a group of fossils, some of which had been brought to this site from at least twenty five miles away. These finds point not only to the more frequent adoption of burial ritual but also to the increasing appearance of personal belongings and personal adornment. Teeth and sea shells perforated at one end were presumably used to make necklaces, and a variety of flint scrapers, borers and awls suggest extensive working of skins to use for clothing, as do awls and needles made of bone.

The increased use of bone is one particularly notable feature of the material belongings of these people. It was used for ritual objects, tools, tallies, and weapons, and represents the first craft, other than flint-working, for which we have reliable evidence. The flint-work of these late Ice-Age hunters is also distinctive, and includes large numbers of angular blades which in form and technique, though not in size, already seem to foreshadow the products of the post-glacial hunters and fishers of Britain. In spite of the development of a new craft (boneworking), of the making and wearing of simple ornaments, and of funerary and possibly other ritual, there can be no doubt that the hunters who lived in the caves of Mendip, Derbyshire, Wales and the South-West penisula, still spent most of their time in the acquisition of food. Although we assume that they gathered some plants, the bulk of their food must have come from animals, and these are attested in the accumulated occupation debris in the caves. Horse-meat may have been the most common meat consumed, but reindeer and mammoth also contributed to the diet and so, it appears, did hares and birds. These latter are unlikely to have been caught with spears or clubs, and so it seems likely that traps of some sort were being used by the end of the last Ice Age. This should not surprise us, for some of the earlier cave paintings from the Dordogne in Southern France appear to show animals whose feet are caught in traps, and we could not expect any evidence of the traps themselves to survive except under very exceptional circumstances.

Apart from the possible use of traps, the pursuit and killing of larger animals was now aided by a new weapon, the bone or antler-barbed point, sometimes called a harpoon head. Examples from Mendip and Devon have barbs down two sides, but points with barbs on one edge only are also known at this period and two were recently found at Poulton le Fylde near Blackpool. This discovery was of particular interest because the two points were found in association with the complete skeleton of an elk, and one of them was still in position in a wound in the animal's hind leg. We can be quite sure therefore that these small weapons, measuring only four of five inches in length, were used to attack large animals.

The careful examination of the elk and the situation in which it was found allows us to picture, in some detail, what a hunt was like in about 10,000 BC. This particular hunt took place in mid-winter, in an area of mixed rough grassland, shrubs and birch wood. The animal, an adult male elk, was initially attacked and wounded a week or so before death. These wounds were found in the rear legs of the animal, and were caused by the bone points, probably attached to arrows and fired by a bow. It looks very much as if there was a deliberate, skilful and successful attempt to reduce the mobility of the animal. Presumably it was then tracked over a period of several days until the hunters were able to move in for the kill. This time they attacked the body, almost certainly with flint-tipped arrows or spears, and some got close enough to the wounded animal to attack it with flint axes, or stones. In this particular instance, however, the hunters were deprived of their prey at the last moment, the animal summoned sufficient strength to break loose and attempted to escape across a nearby lake which at this time of year was almost certainly iced over around its margins. Either the ice gave way, or the animal, attempting to swim to safety, was too weak to succeed; in any event he died there and his carcass eventually drifted to the lake side and was engulfed in sediments which preserved the skeleton intact until the present day.

This episode, which must have been in many ways typical of hunting expeditions all over Southern Britain, took place at the very end of the Ice Age and we find the post-glacial hunters pursuing the same prey with the same weapons. These people, however, often known as Maglemosians, were living in a world which was changing in several respects.

Harpoon head from Aveline's Hole.

Around 8,500 BC there was a marked rise in temperatures which encouraged the rapid spread of forest, at first of birch and pine, and then of hazel, oak and elm as well. The horse, bison, reindeer and mammoth disappeared from the landscape as conditions became increasingly unsuitable for them, and they were replaced by animals who thrived in woodland — deer, elk, wild oxen (aurochs), and wild boar. But these animals were less inclined to move in herds, and the woodland generally supported fewer of these large creatures than did the open tundra and grasslands. Food animals therefore became scarcer and more difficult to catch, while at the same time the hunting grounds were partially diminished as the ice melted and the sea level rose. By 6,000 BC Britain was an island, and in the long term this was probably the most important change of all.

The new conditions are reflected in the tool-kits and weapons of the Maglemosian hunters. Heavy flint axes which could be resharpened quickly and with comparative ease by blows struck across their cutting edge were introduced to enable the increased forest to be better exploited. At the same time large numbers of small, angular blades (microliths) were produced and used as the barbs and points of arrows. They were fixed, with resin made from birch bark, to wooden shafts which, on the evidence of preserved examples from Denmark, were more than three feet long and equipped with feathered flights. Their bows, of elm or yew, were up to seven feet long, and in addition to flint tipped and barbed arrows also fired those tipped with the bone points already mentioned earlier. Spears with bone or antler heads completed the armoury, which overall shows great improvements in medium and long range weapons over those used towards the end of the Ice Age. It was, of course, precisely these types of weapon which were most needed to successfully hunt the animals of the forest.

The Maglemosians also compensated for the greater scarcity of food-animals and the greater difficulty in catching them, by exploiting other sources of food. We know that they gathered fruits and nuts in season, and almost certainly vegetables too, although no evidence of these survives. At the same time they realised that rich supplies of food could be harvested from lakes, rivers and the sea. Around lake-sides fowl were caught, while by the sea, a variety of sea-birds provided an important source of meat. At Morton, in Fife, nine species of such birds were represented amongst the food-remains of hunters who lived

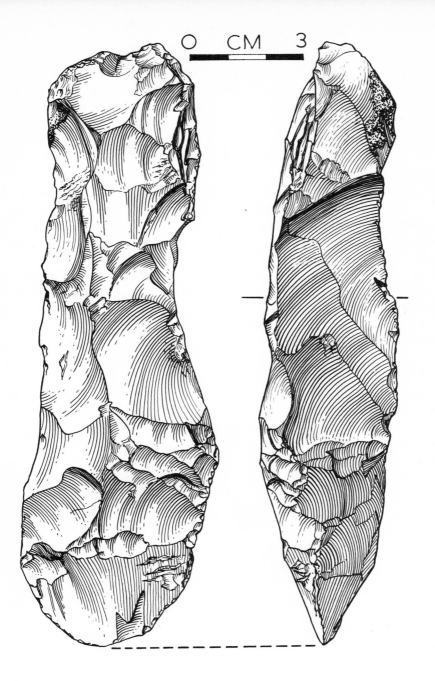

A core-axe used by post-glacial hunters, from Ley Hill, Herts.

here about 5,000 BC; the guillemot and the gannet seem to have been particularly favoured, though this may mean simply that they were more numerous or easier to catch. The same people who caught and ate these birds also consumed large quantities of fish and other seafood, particularly cod, crab and cockles. At the same time they seem to have been able to catch deer, wild ox, and boar in the vicinity of their camp site, and these animals still provided the bulk of their meat, probably about two thirds of it.

Despite their skill and enterprise in utilising all the available resources of the area, however, the site at Morton was not occupied permanently or even for a substantial part of the year. It seems to have been used for a short period during the autumn, between summer hunting in the hills and winter hunting in the more protected lowland areas further inland. Short-lived, seasonal occupation of sites was still the pattern throughout Britain, although the occupation of some sites may have extended over a longer period of each year than had ever been the case during the Ice Ages.

This is suggested by the accumulating evidence that the Maglemosians were prepared to spend considerable effort in constructing shelters and occupation areas for themselves. The most notable example is the site of Star Carr in Yorkshire, where, about 8000 BC, a group of hunters chopped down birch trees on the edge of a marshy lake and used them as the base of an earth and brushwood platform. This seems to have been used largely as a working area, suggesting that there is an undiscovered occupation site nearby, and many interesting tools and implements were found here. At Morton several shelters were erected on solid wooden stakes, the largest shelter measuring about seven feet by four feet, with an entrance at one end and a hearth by the door. In the Southern Pennines at Broomhead Moor stake holes and stone alignments associated with concentrations of flint work are the remains of a shelter built and used about 6700 BC. At Sheldon, in the same region, a natural rock shelter had been improved by the introduction of a roughly cobbled floor and the construction of a stone platform. Further south, and on present evidence later in time, several groups of hunters dug roughly oblong pits two or three feet down into the soil and probably roofed them over with branches covered by skins or bracken. Examples from Wawcott (Berks), Farnham and Abinger (Surrey) and Selmeston (Sussex) have occasional post and stake holes

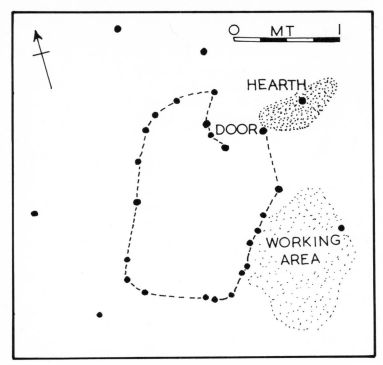

The remains of a temporary hut of c.6,700 BC at Morton, Fife.

which may have supported the main rafter of such a roof, as well as hearths and flint tools and debris on the ground surface outside the shelters. None of these structures could justly be described as a house, or even a hut, but they show, just as much as the new tools and weapons and the new food sources which were exploited, that by this time man was consciously seeking both to make the best of his natural environment and to improve his material comfort.

At the same time they provide some hint of social developments. The number of people using Star Carr is thought to have been about fifteen to twenty, while at Morton it is estimated that ten or twelve people occupied the site at any one time. At Farnham four occupation pits were excavated and there was evidence that several others existed, although not all may have been in use at once. These communities of ten to twenty people did not yet, as far as we know, support any specialist craftsmen, but the first steps towards specialisation were perhaps taking place. Bone and antler played an increasingly important part in the material culture of these people, and were used to make awls, needles, harpoon heads, spearheads, scoops, pins, fish-hooks, chisels and mattocks. Some small flint cutting tools seem to have been made specifically for use in cutting and working antler and bone. At the same time wood was becoming a craft material, for making bows, arrows, and traps, as well as being cut and roughly shaped to provide supports for shelters. At Star Carr a wooden paddle was found, and from Friarton, near Perth, came a dug-out canoe of the type which might have been propelled by it. The fishermen of Morton must have used a boat too, since some of the fish they caught could only be found in deeper water. Although all of these things may have been made by any or all of the community it seems likely that those who showed special skills and aptitudes in working one material or the other would have tended to work mainly in that medium, possibly with the encouragement of the others in the group.

One field of activity in which special abilities might have seemed to come to the fore was in dealings with the supernatural. The rich cave paintings of France and Spain show that by the end of the Ice Age European man had developed a belief in the supernatural, and almost certainly in ways to combat or treat with it. Some of these paintings appear to show men dressed in animal skins and wearing antlers or masks, and although these may have been attempts to decoy animals they may also represent the first medicine-men, witch-doctors or priests, whichever one prefers to call them. Several masks made from the skulls and antlers of deer were found at Star Carr and may be surviving evidence of the activities of such men. At the same time as these developments were taking place within these small hunting communities, relationships were being established with other groups, both human and animal. The population of the country, though almost certainly growing, was still sparse and in most areas contact cannot have been frequent. For this very reason there was probably little friction between groups and such contacts as existed may have been more friendly than hostile. Some objects probably changed hands occasionally, and the block of Baltic amber found in Aveline's Hole on Mendip seems likely to have found its way by barter or exchange from the east coast of England to Somerset. More interesting however are the results of recent research in Dorset on the exploitation of Portland

28

chert. By about 4500 BC, this useful material was being used for implements in Gloucestershire, West Cornwall and Sussex, as well as many areas nearer to Portland. How this material was moved over these distances we still do not know, but occupation of Portland at this period seems to have been sufficiently dense to suggest that local hunting groups may have been able to lay claim to this resource and barter it further afield. Further research and discoveries may allow us to identify the mechanism by which the chert was 'traded'.

The various trends, which were developing between 8000 and 4000 BC, that is towards slightly less temporary shelters and settlement, towards specialisation and barter, and a more intensive exploitation of natural resources, were all to pave the way for the next important phase in Britain's prehistory. They were joined by one further development: the first attempts to control animal population. The hunters of Star Carr already possessed, before 7000 BC, the domesticated dog, the first animal to be trained to serve man. The excavators of the elk at Poulton le Fylde suggested that the initial intention of his attackers had perhaps been to immobilise him and capture him alive. In this way they may have been able to have kept him, alive, until they needed a fresh supply of meat. At some occupation sites of this period the evidence of the animal bones suggests that the animals must have been killed close to the camp, where their complete carcasses were butchered. The camps may have been unusually well sited for just this purpose, but it is also possible that animals were caught and kept penned near the camp sites until they were needed. Of these possibilities we can say no more, but it does seem that as time passed post-glacial hunters, gatherers and fishers in Britain may have grown increasingly adept at controlling their food supply. In this, as in other achievements, they had come a long way from those first hunters who had set foot in Britain a quarter of a million years before.

4,000–2,700 BC

It is possible, even probable, that had the post-glacial hunters of Britain been left to their own devices they would, in time, have domesticated some of the indigenous wild species such as the wild ox and the wild pig, and created an economy based on animal-rearing instead of hunting. In the event, however, animal husbandry and farming in general, were introduced to the British Isles by newcomers from the continent of Europe. At present, the earliest traces of these immigrants have been found at Ballynagilly in Tyrone, where pits and a hearth attest to their presence by about 3,900 BC. Other occupation sites are dated, by C.14, to the period from about 3,500 BC onwards, but we can be quite sure that these new arrivals had spread widely throughout much of Britain and Ireland by this time, for some of the monuments erected then already overlay land which had been cleared and either cultivated or used as pastureland. Taken together, the evidence of archaeology and of botany, suggests that in the centuries from about 4,000 BC to 3,600 BC small groups of people set sail from the west coast of Europe and crossed the Channel and the North Sea to settle and farm in Britain. As far as we can judge, these people all used much the same sort of tools and equipment, grew the same crops and reared the same animals. Thus, though they spread out on reaching Britain they brought a certain uniformity of human activity and human culture to the island. At the same time, the way of life which they introduced was quite different to that of the existing population, for they were farmers who grew crops as well as raised animals, and so they led an altogether more settled existence.

When they first arrived in Britain, of course, they found an island which was thickly forested, and where good pasture and agricultural land had to be created before it could be used. From the ancient plant remains preserved in the soil, we can see that the new settlers began work immediately, clearing away the forest either with fire or with the improved flint axes which they used. Experiments have shown that

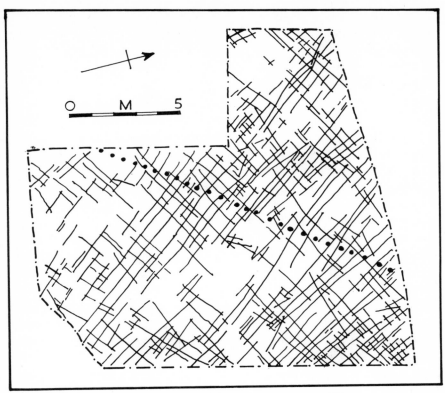

Fields and plough-marks of about 3,000 BC at South Street, Wilts.

with these sharper tools, three men could clear six hundred square yards of birch wood in only four hours. With the trees felled, the roots removed, and the larger stones taken away, some of the cleared land was then used to sow crops. The ground was ploughed, in two directions (cross-ploughing), presumably with a wooden plough of which we have no surviving evidence. Plough marks of this sort found at South Street in Wiltshire were each up to forty feet long and suggest that the plough was pulled by an ox. Here there were traces of a wooden fence which may have enclosed separate fields, whilst at Behy-Glenulra and Belderg Beg in Western Ireland cultivated fields were found to be enclosed by stone walls. Within these fields crops of wheat and barley, and occasionally a little flax, were sown. Wheat was the favoured crop, particularly a variety known as emmer, but barley was

31

also grown in small quantities. When the crop was ripe it was harvested with sickles of which only the flint teeth survive, but which were probably short and almost straight. The crop was then stored either in jars or in small pits dug into the ground. These pits are one of the most characteristic features of the settlements of these farmers, and are often very numerous. At Hurst Fen in East Anglia there were over two hundred of them, many arranged in groups of ten to fifteen at a time. When the corn was to be used for baking, it was taken and ground on stone querns, mill stones shaped either like a saucer or a saddle.

The land which was not used for crops came under grass and supported ox, sheep and goat. At the same time domesticated pigs were run in the forest. The cattle had long horns, and were descended from the wild aurochs, and the sheep were characterised by goat-like horns, long tails, and a coarse wool which never seems to have been spun or woven. Food remains reveal that all of these animals were overwintered in considerable numbers, though how they were fed through the winter is still unknown. Of all these animals cattle were certainly the most important, and at Windmill Hill in Wiltshire they may have made up almost two-thirds of all the animals consumed. Sheep and pig were initially of roughly equal importance, but growing numbers of sheep suggest that as more land was cleared the importance of the pig declined. The most important feature shown by the food remains however, is the scarcity of wild animals. Although the relative importance of cattle, sheep and pig probably varied from one settlement to another, that of domesticated and wild animals appears to have been much the same everywhere, with domesticated animals predominating. The keeping of sheep and cattle and, even more, the growing of crops, meant that these people had to lead a more settled life than that of the hunters and fishers, but at the same time gave them the ability to do so. They had a food supply which they could control and manipulate, and wherever they found suitable land to farm they could settle down to occupy the site permanently. This does not mean that farmsteads necessarily grew up and thrived in the same spot for centuries, but that many sites were now occupied by the same family throughout the year, and for several years, even decades, at a time.

Many of these settlements seem to be no more than the farmsteads of a single family. Isolated huts have been found at Ballynagilly, Haldon, Corfe Mullen, Fengate and elsewhere, and pairs of huts at Clegyr

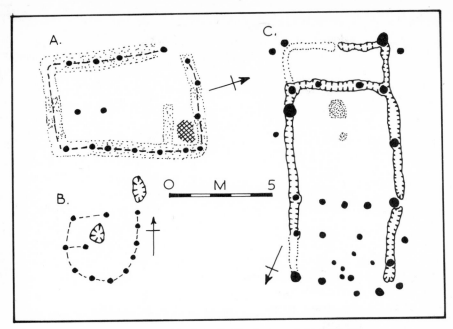

Houses of early farmers at A. Haldon, B. Henbury and C. Ballyglass.

Boia in Pembrokeshire and Eaton Heath in Norfolk. Some of these huts are rectangular, others circular, and yet others oval or apsidal. In contrast to the overall uniformity of pottery and flint tools, houses and the methods used to build them vary greatly, even in a single region. In size these huts are rarely much larger than the living-room of a modern house. The huts at Fengate and Ballynagilly were each nearly twenty feet square, whilst that at Haldon measured about twenty five feet by sixteen feet. They were, in modern terms, bed-sitters, with little evidence of any attempt to provide privacy for the family. Most of them have a hearth inside, but other hearths are often found outside and this is where cooking was probably done in fine weather. Equally, concentrations of flint tools are often thickest not inside the huts but immediately around them, and we may assume that working with flints, bone, wood and leather was all done outside rather than in the darkness of the hut's interior.

Although they were small, most of these huts were quite substantial buildings which would have stood up well to the British weather.

The "causewayed camp" at Windmill Hill, Wilts.

Many were erected on a framework of timber uprights sunk into post-holes, like that found at Ballyglass in Western Ireland, or that at Haldon. Others seem to have employed horizontal timber planking, like the oak planks used at Ballynagilly, or slots cut into the gound, into which wall panels could be bedded. This was the method used at Fengate. As for the wall panels themselves, these may have been of further horizontal planking or of wattle, which was daubed with clay and straw. Almost certainly the roofs were of thatch, possibly on brush-wood, which in most cases was arranged with a ridge running along the long axis of the building. A few sites have produced evidence of this sort of building grouped in settlements which appear to be larger and more populous than individual farmsteads. At Ascott-under-Wychwood, for example, concentrations of pottery and flintwork sug-gest the former presence of several huts, and at Hurst Fen traces of occupation cover an area measuring about 180 by 90 yds, enclosed on at least two sides by ditches. The presence of two hundred pits as well as stake holes, and the high density of artifacts — flint tools and pottery in particular — strongly suggest that this was the site of a sizeable settlement, even though no recognisable hut plans can be traced. The other evidence for communities larger than the isolated farmstead comes from some of the sites occupied now or slightly later by the so-called 'causewayed camps'. At Henbury in Devon the end of a spur was enclosed by eight short lengths of ditch, separated by irregular causeways and backed by a bank composed of the soil thrown up from the ditches. Inside this area there were storage pits, cooking hollows, hearths and flimsy traces of huts with curving walls. In addition, near to the entrance, there was a more substantial apsidal hut, erected on a framework of seventeen timber uprights. But there was also occupation outside this enclosure, and traces of a second ditch with a palisade, and there is the possibility that the permanent occupation of the site and the building and use of the causewayed camp were not one and the same thing. At Windmill Hill in Wiltshire another causewayed camp was quite certainly preceded by earlier occupation of the site. Again the characteristic pits were found and there were post-holes suggestive of the presence of huts; in two places close to the ditches of the later camp, alignments of post-holes might be the remains of rectangular huts partially obliterated by the digging of the causewayed ditches.

These traces of more extensive settlements, and their occurrence on the sites of causewayed camps is of some significance because the camps themselves provide evidence for the emergence of social units or groupings larger than that of the family alone. About twenty of these camps are now known, and others almost certainly await discovery. They are spread across Southern England, and are characterised by their roughly circular enclosures demarcated by the causewayed ditches and accompanying banks. The ditches seem to have been important largely as quarries for the bank material and were often used as rubbish tips shortly after they were dug. A few of the camps have only the one ring of ditches, but many have two or three roughly concentric rings and this is so at the best known of these sites, Windmill Hill. Here, three rings enclose a total area of about twenty-one acres. Had these twenty-one acres been filled with remains of huts and other occupation features we should have evidence of a very large community indeed, but here and at most other causewayed camps which have been sampled by excavation, it is clear that these enclosures were not really camps at all and were not occupied for any length of time but probably visited seasonally. Henbury may be an exception to this rule, but at Windmill Hill the main traces of domestic occupation are dated to about 3100 BC and the digging of the causewayed ditches to 2700 BC. On the other hand, Windmill Hill is certainly not the earliest of the causewayed camps, since apart from Henbury (c.3500 BC), the camps at Abingdon are dated by C.14 to c.3300 BC, and those at Hambledon Hill and Knap Hill to about 2900 BC.

It is now generally agreed that these so-called camps were in fact places where communal gatherings took place, probably in the spring and the autumn. At Windmill Hill the burial of complete animals may imply ritual or sacrificial burials, and the appearance here of stone tools made of material available no nearer than Bath or Frome suggests that some visitors to the site came from considerable distances.

A leaf-shaped arrowhead of c.3,000 BC.

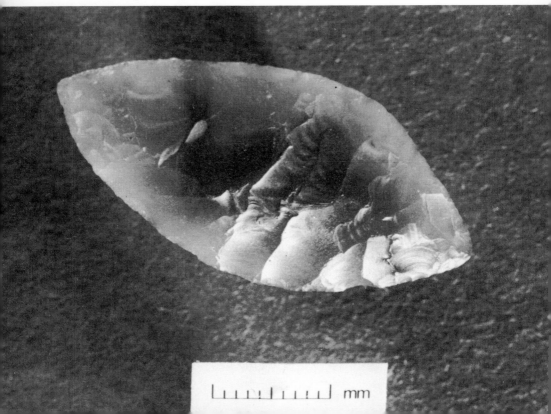

mm

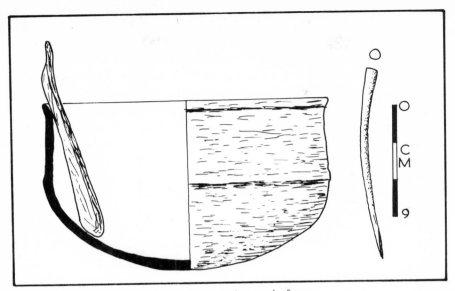

Pottery bowl, wooden porridge stirrer, and yew pin from
the Sweet Track, Soms, c.3,000 BC.

Taken together with the communal effort which the construction of
such camps demanded, estimated in the case of Windmill Hill as perhaps 120,000 man hours, the evidence suggests the emergence of what,
for want of a better word, we might call tribes. Equally the widely
spaced distribution of most of the camps, and the evidence of visitors
from many miles away at Windmill Hill, raises the possibility that
these tribes each inhabited and exploited a territory which they
regarded as their own. To what extent these social developments are
confined to Southern England is uncertain, but two sites in Ireland, at
Lyles Hill and Goodland, might possibly point to similar developments there. Both are circular enclosures which have produced pottery, stone axes and flint work of about 3000 BC without any firm
traces of accompanying huts or other permanent structures. At the
same time the stone walled fields and enclosures at Behy-Glenulra
point very clearly to the growth of large settled communities in Western Ireland. Already over two hundred acres of neatly laid out enclosures have been discovered, attesting both to the size of the
community involved and to their social organisation.

37

From these same sites, in both Ireland and England, we have evidence that as the social unit grew larger, so certain individuals assumed greater importance. There is some evidence, from the funerary monuments erected for them, that many local chieftains emerged but what form their leadership took and how they rose to it we cannot say. On the other hand, we can now identify a number of specialists whose role in society is reasonably clear. Almost certainly these specialists included potters and flint-workers, the former producing dark, polished bowls with wide mouths and rounded bases, and the latter a wide range of tools from small scrapers, knives and awls, to superbly made leaf and lozenge shaped arrowheads, sickle flints and polished flint axes. Outside the areas where flint could be obtained from the chalk, axes were made of hard volcanic rocks which were certainly extracted and shaped by specialists in the craft. Both flint and stone axes were no longer held directly in the hand but were now inserted into wooden hafts, a few of which have fortunately survived with the axe-head still in place. The making of hafts may well have been part of a specialist craft itself for in the peat of the Somerset Levels archaeologists are now recovering many examples of wooden objects made between about 3400 and 2700 BC, as well as those of later date. They range from weapons such as spears, bows of yew, and flint arrowheads still fixed in their wooden shafts, through the larger wooden implements such as paddles, clubs and digging sticks, to small tools and clothing accessories such as dishes, handles, pins and toggles. Perhaps the most interesting find was a broken pottery bowl and an associated 'porridge' stirrer (or spurtle) of wood; unfortunately the porridge itself was not preserved!

Apart from these many products of the carpenter's craft, the peat also covers constructed trackways which attest both to the quality of craftsmanship available by this time, and to the amount of labour which went into their making. The earliest track yet discovered, called the Sweet Track, is dated to about 3100 BC, and was soon followed by the construction of other tracks. Unlike later tracks, the Sweet Track was built like a catwalk, with timber rails laid end-to-end and fixed in position with hundreds of sharpened pegs of holly, hazel and alder. Peat was then packed over the rails, and oak planks were bedded onto the peat and tied down by further pegs driven vertically into the peat and through carefully made notches in the ends of the planks. Some of

A detail of the catwalk of the Sweet Track.

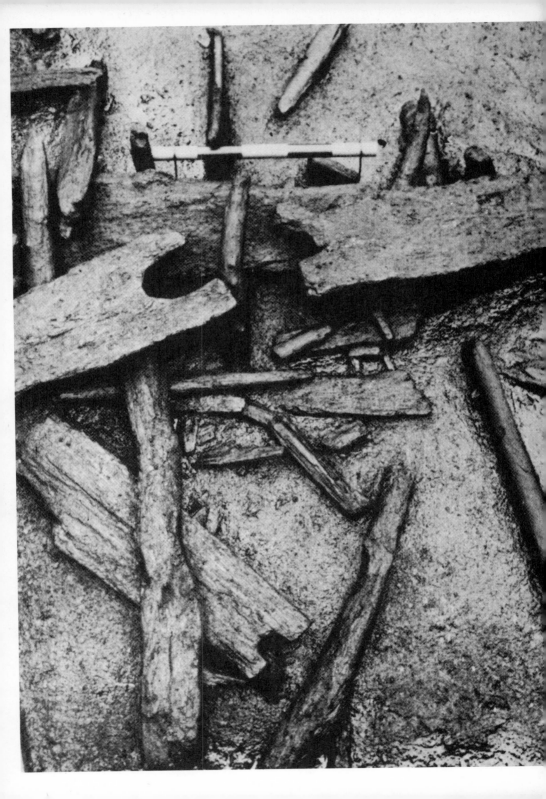

the slightly later tracks, built about 2,950 BC, were wider than this and used birch or hazel brushwood and wands spread to a width of about five feet to form the basis of a sound trackway. Where these tracks were going and who or what travelled along them is not yet clear, but already several miles of trackway have been traced and more await discovery.

Elsewhere in Britain there were 'trackways' in use by this time, but these were not built or laid but were simply routeways along which people moved from one area to another. Exactly when they came into use is unkown, and it is possible that some of these routes were already pioneered and used by the late post-glacial hunters. It was the farmers and craftsmen who gradually replaced them, however, who had most need of such trackways, for some of the raw materials they used were only available in certain locations. We now know that flint, stone axes, pottery and probably jet were all trade goods by about 3000 BC or shortly after. Jet, from the Whitby district of Yorkshire, became more important as a material for necklace beads and other small items

The Berkshire Ridgeway west of Uffington.

later on, and was probably not an important item of trade at this time, but its occasional appearance is Southern and Eastern England reveals the wide contacts which were possible by 3000 BC. Pottery, perhaps because it was both heavy and fragile, was not traded over such great distances but occasionally travelled as much as 200 miles from its source. In particular, pottery produced near the Lizard in Cornwall is found not only on many sites in the south-west peninsula but as far east as Corfe Mullen (Dorset) and Windmill Hill. Whether it was traded as a commodity in its own right or as a container for some other valuable material such as salt, is uncertain but the pottery itself was certainly popular. Local potters in Dorset and Wiltshire copied the Cornish vases, and copies produced in the Bath and Frome district were themselves traded in some quantity into Wiltshire.

What was exchanged for the pottery or its contents is also unknown, but one important product of Southern and Eastern England was flint. The fine flintwork now being produced, and particularly the large polished flint axes, utilised not surface flints but fresh

Two polished flint axes, c.3,000 BC.

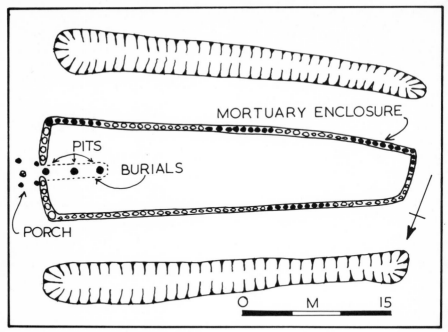

The earthen long barrow at Fussell's Lodge.

nodules which had to be extracted from the flint seams in the chalk. By 3500 BC the first flint miners were digging their shafts at Findon in Sussex, and other Sussex flint mines came into use shortly afterwards at Blackpatch, Harrow Hill and Cissbury. Later, flint mining was carried out in Wiltshire and East Anglia. In all of these mines the chalk was removed by the use of antler picks and rakes, and shovels made from the shoulder blade of the wild aurochs (ox). The nodules of flint were hauled to the surface and there roughly shaped. Secondary shaping very often also took place at the mines, but finishing and polishing seems to have been done elsewhere, possibly at the time and place that an exchange was made. On present evidence the flint-miners did not occupy the mine sites permanently, and mining itself may have been a seasonal occupation. Having obtained the rough-outs of axes and other supplies of flint, it was probably the miners themselves who then traded their products with the farmers of the chalk uplands of Southern and Eastern England. Hoards of axes, such as one from Peaslake

The facade of the megalithic tomb of Waylands Smithy, Berks.

(Surrey), probably represent the activities of these artisans. The flint-miners, however, faced increasing competition from axe-producers living in the north and west of Britain. Here, where flint could not be mined from the chalk, volcanic rocks were used to make hard, finely-polished axes. Well before 3000 BC axe factories of this type were beginning to appear in Cornwall, Pembrokeshire, the Lake District and in Northern Ireland at Tievebulliagh. Others appeared later, and the major period of activity in all these factories falls in the period between 2700 and 2000 BC. Nevertheless, some early axes from Cornish and Irish factories found their way over considerable distances including axes from Langdale found in Northern Ireland and East Anglian and Cornish axes discovered at Windmill Hill.

Contact between highland and lowland zones in Britain, and between the British mainland and Ireland, is revealed not only by the movement of stone axes but also by the widespread appearance of similar — but not identical — types of tomb and funerary practises. The

43

A model of the megalithic tomb at Stoney Littleton, Soms.

earliest tombs used by the immigrant farmers were on present evidence, the earthen long barrows found in Southern and Eastern England. Several of these were in use by about 3500 BC, including one example from Dalladies north of the Tay estuary in Eastern Scotland. Slightly later examples are known from Yorkshire and South-West Scotland as well as others from Wessex. These tombs are remarkably uniform in type, comprising trapezoidal mounds usually between 100 and 400 feet long, with the burials grouped in a tiny area at the broad, eastern end of the barrow. Many have traces of structures beneath the barrow, built of turf, stones or timber. Some of these are enclosures almost as big as the barrow itself, in which it is thought the bodies of the dead may have been exposed before final burial. Others are small mortuary houses in which the bodies may have been laid during the

The entrance to the megalithic tomb at Nympsfield, Glos.

funerary period, the clearest examples being those found at Dalladies, Wayland's Smithy (Berks) and Nutbane (Hants).

Wayland's Smithy is a particularly important monument because here the earthen long barrow was overlaid, shortly after 3000 BC, by a longer mound of similar shape and orientation, but incorporating at the broad end an arrangement of three built stone chambers which open off a central passage. The whole of the mound is surrounded by a stone kerb, and the front of the tomb is transformed into an impressive façade by alternating megaliths and panels of drystone walling. This type of tomb is found in greater numbers further west in the Cotswolds and South-East Wales, where several of the tombs have a small V-shaped courtyard in front of the entrance. In some cases the entrances which lie at the rear of these courtyards are completely false; behind

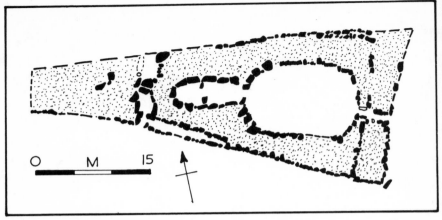

The court cairn at Creevykeel, Sligo.

the drystone walling and megaliths there are no burial chambers, which in fact are set further back in the mound and entered from the side. One of the best known of these tombs, at West Kennet in Wiltshire, is unusual, having a larger, U-shaped courtyard before its chambers and this suggests a connection with tombs of basically the same sort found in South-West Scotland and in Ireland. These tombs are the same shape as those of southern and western England, and like them they are surrounded by stone kerbs and have a façade of megaliths and drystone walling behind which are stone built burial chambers. The chambers themselves, however, are usually a straight row of two to four rectangular compartments separated by slabs projecting from the side walls and/or floor, while the forecourts are much more elaborate than those of the English tombs.

In Scotland the forecourts are often U-shaped like that of West Kennet, but in Ireland many forecourts are three-quarters or totally enclosed by two projecting 'horns' of the barrow. Some archaeologists have aptly called them 'lobster-claw' cairns for this reason. A well preserved example is still to be seen at Creevykeel. In spite of these differences, however, the Irish, Scottish and English long-barrows with stone kerbs, façades and chambers are closely related and variants on a single theme, all apparently making their appearance shortly before 3000 BC. Almost certainly they represent the translation into stone of the tomb-type represented by the earthen long-barrows, and in the case of Ireland and Scotland this would mean contacts with other

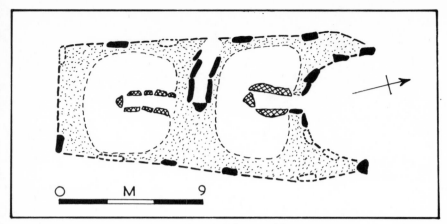

The megalithic tomb at Mid Gleniron I, Wigtownshire.

parts of the British Isles at this time. Where the people of Ireland and western and northern Scotland buried their dead until they adopted or developed the megalithic long barrow, however, remains to be demonstrated, for at present C.14 dates suggest that these areas were occupied for five hundred years and more before the earliest long barrows were erected. In Ireland there is no certain evidence for earlier burial places, though some Irish archaeologists believe that much simpler megalithic tombs comprising a single chamber fronted by impressive portal stones may have been used. On the other hand, in Scotland there are now several long barrows which are known to overlie and contain earlier round ones. These earlier round tombs usually have either a short passage-cum-burial chamber, or a passage which opens into a square or polygonal compartment. The classic site is at Mid-Gleniron in Wigtownshire, where two such barrows were built and used before being covered and incorporated into a megalithic long barrow, with its U-shaped forecourt.

These forecourts were used for funerary and post-funerary rituals which appear to have included feasting, the deposition of offerings, and no doubt other activities which have left no trace for the archaeologist. The hearths which were used during these rites are often found, and at Cairnholy in Galloway six such hearths matched exactly the number of burials originally made in the tomb. Elsewhere the various megalithic long barrows usually contain the remains of between five and twenty people. These comparatively small numbers, when com-

47

pared with the effort required to build the tombs and move the stones used in their construction, at once raises the question, for whom were the tombs built? There is no firm evidence which allows us to answer this question, but the number and distribution of these tombs, together with the command of a sizeable labour force which they seem to imply, suggests that they were the tombs of local chieftains and their families. A careful study of the skeletal remains from a tomb at Lanhill (Wilts) suggested that nine skulls belonged to members of a single family, and some family relationship was postulated amongst the dead buried in West Kennet. Similarly ten individuals buried in an earthen long barrow at Skendleby (Lincs) were thought to be related to one another. In view of the fact that these tombs seem to have been open and in use for centuries, these suggested relationships certainly seem to imply that we are dealing with the burials of an elite.

Towards the end of our period this conclusion is strengthened by the appearance of massive circular mounds covering a single burial chamber approached by a long passage. The passage and chamber are built of great megaliths many of which carry elaborate decoration. Around the base of the mound the stone kerb includes many stones similarly decorated. These tombs, of which the two prime examples are at New Grange and Knowth in Ireland were, for a long time thought to be brought to the western seaboard by immigrants or even 'missionaries' from Iberia or the Mediterranean. The discovery of the earlier circular barrows such as Gleniron, and the general development of megalithic tombs and architecture prior to 3000 BC, now makes it possible to see these tombs as the supreme products of an indigenous development. At the same time as they were being built other important monuments were perhaps beginning to appear for the first time, for the earliest of the so-called 'henge monuments' may be dated to about 2700 BC. Alongside these developments there were other changes taking place which, although they happened over a considerable length of time, seem to emerge in recognisable form in the same period. New types of pottery, flintwork, and bonework make their appearance, new axe factories go into production, and new trends in farming can perhaps be detected. All in all, the evidence suggests that by about 2700 BC, the initial spread of the farmers and the consolidation of their hold on the land was complete, and the prehistory of Britain was about to enter a new phase.

2,700–2,200 BC

For many years, the changes which can be detected taking place after the initial arrival, spread and settlement of the first farmers in Britain, were seen as the results of the mixing, and to some extent the fusion, of the indigenous culture of the hunters with the immigrant culture of the farmers. The heavier, coarser pottery, the increased interest in working bone and antler, and the appearance of new flint-working techniques and implements were all believed to represent the end-products of such a process. Equally the scant and flimsy traces of huts found in association with these things, and the coastal and riverside distribution of sites producing them, supported the notion that these various artifacts were made and used by people who had emerged from a hunting and fishing society. We can now see that this process did not, in fact, take place, except perhaps in Ireland. Elsewhere the indigenous hunters and fishers must gradually have died out, initially retreating perhaps from the areas where the farmers settled, their numbers gradually diminishing as the forests which provided their hunting grounds were slowly cleared. Exactly how and when they disappeared from the British landscape we cannot say, but it is clear that they made little or no contribution to the societies occupying Britain from about 3000 BC onwards. Our new view of the period from about 2,700 to 2,000 BC is one which recognises both continuity and change. There was little change, for example, in the size and form of settlements. Types of pottery in use gradually evolved in both form and decoration, and many of the impressive monuments erected in the preceding era were still frequented and used. At the same time there were changes of emphasis in the role of certain crafts and industries, there were new trends in farming, and there was the development of new types of ritual and funerary monuments together with changing emphasis on various burial practises. Finally, the comparative uniformity of pottery, crafts, architecture, and, to a certain degree, funerary monuments in the period between 4,000 and 2,700 BC was partially broken down in the following five hundred years as regional groupings of all these things became more pronounced.

At the same time the area of human occupation seems to have expanded, if our present distribution maps may be taken as broadly correct. South-East England, for example, was comparatively neglected by the early farmers except for occupation near the coast, whereas, from about 2,700 BC, it seems to have been quite densely occupied. Similarly the East and South-East Midlands were now opened up to farming. Almost certainly this expansion of the farmed and occupied areas of Britian represents growing population. Not only are there many more known occupation sites of this period and new areas of settlement, but in areas already being farmed there is a pronounced increase in the density of occupation in this period. Recent work at Fengate in the Nene Valley has revealed a growing number and density of sites as well as an expansion of the settled area. This growth of population was almost certainly due not to further arrivals of farmers from the Continent but to the increasing success of those already here in exploiting the land to the full.

We still have remarkably little evidence, however, of the settlements in which these farmers lived, particularly in Southern England. Some of the earliest discoveries of their occupation sites were made at Peterborough and Grovehurst (Kent) and in each case revealed roughly circular hollows, about twelve feet across, containing occupation debris. The absence of any substantial post-holes for timber superstructures has inevitably led to the suggestion that these were flimsy huts of inferior size and strength to those used by the earlier farmers. Although this is not necessarily true for there are ways of constructing very substantial timber buildings without sinking posts into the ground, we have to admit that on present evidence there was perhaps a change in both building techniques and in the basic shape of the huts, for the evidence from other sites in Yorkshire, Wiltshire and Bedfordshire also points to a preference for the circular plan which, though used in the earlier period, was less common then than the rectangular one. Circular huts are found further west in this period too, at New Grange and Lough Gur in Ireland, while the earliest structure erected at The Sanctuary, Overton Hill (Wilts) was a circular timber hut about 15 feet in diameter. The general trend might perhaps be reflected in the circular timber buildings, of very much greater size, which are built not long

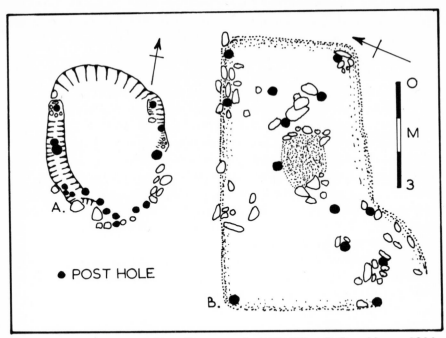

Houses of c.2,700 BC at A. New Grange, and c.2,200 BC at B. Ronaldsway, IOM.

after 2200 BC inside some of the great ceremonial sites of Southern England. Certainly these buildings imply a lengthy tradition of substantial circular buildings which preceded their erection. It would be quite wrong, however, to suggest that there was a sudden switch from rectangular to circular and oval buildings; rather there was a trend towards the latter, a change in fashion if you like, the reasons for which we cannot appreciate. Rectangular buildings certainly continued to be erected, as we know from sites of this period in Western Britain. The huts around Lough Gur, for example, included rectangular as well as circular ones, some of them over 30 feet long. A hut almost as large was found at Glencrutchery (I.O.M.) and another slightly smaller at Ronaldsway (I.O.M.). On the mainland of Britain, sub-rectangular and apsidal houses have been discovered at Cefn Cilsanws and Little Paxton (Hunts).

All these latter sites seem to be no more than isolated farmsteads, similar in many respects to those of the first farmers. At Lough Gur, on the other hand, there was an extensive area of settlement, and the same appears to be true of Peterborough and Grovehurst. It would be wrong to call these settlements villages, but there is perhaps the suggestion of farmers coming together and living in close proximity to one another. This might be related to the contemporary trend towards pastoralism, which is indicated by the comparative scarcity of querns or mill stones, on sites of this period, and of the storage pits which characterised the settlement sites of the first farmers. Sickle flints too are much scarcer, and the pottery of this period less frequently contains the impressions of accidentally incorporated grain, such as were quite common on pottery of the preceding era. Bone deposits of the period immediately after 2200 BC reveal that at the same time as pastoralism grew in importance, there was a change in the balance of the animal population. In Southern England cattle became more numerous at the expense of sheep, and pigs replaced sheep as the second most important animal in the farming economy. Both changes might relate, at least in part, to the expansion of settlement onto lower ground and riverside locations, where pasture for cattle was more easily found that grazing for sheep, but where there was still plenty of forest in which the pigs could be run. From what little evidence is available, these trends in Southern England were repeated elsewhere, although in the far north, in the Orkney Islands, sheep maintained their favoured postion in relation to pig, and there is now quite a lot of evidence for the growing of crops, particularly barley.

While these important changes were taking place in the subsistence economy, other fields of economic activity seem to have changed little. All the stone axe factories which had begun production in the earlier period continued and amplified their activities, whilst further factories were established for the first time. These included those at Graig Lwyd (Caernarvon) and in the Penzance district (Cornwall). The actual factory site at Graig Lwyd is well known, and reveals these 'factories' for what they were. Here, on the exposed mountainside, rock was taken from the screes and worked into rough-outs of the tools which were eventually to be produced. No polishing or other finishing of the tools was done here, and there is little evidence of any occupation of the site apart from the occasional hearth or fire-place. At more than two dozen factories all over the highland zone of Britain, similar activities were taking place. The rise in the number of factories, and in the quantity of tools produced, clearly points to a growing demand for these products, possibly because they were preferred to flint axes but also, one suspects, because of the new phase of land clearance which must have come with the expansion of settlement and the growth of population. While factories still found their best markets close at hand, increasing numbers of axes are found hundreds of miles from the factories which produced them. Porcellanite axes from Tievebulliagh in Northern Ireland are found spread from the Orkneys to Dorset and Kent; the axes from Langdale are found from Cornwall to Scotland, East Anglia and Ireland. How these axes and the men who traded them travelled we do not know, but some at least must have been moved by boat, the remains of which have been found occasionally.

The decline of the flint axe in the face of the stone one may be indicated by the declining use of the Sussex and Wessex flint-mines, as well as by the large numbers of imported stone axes found in Wessex. In East Anglia on the other hand, far-removed from any of the axe factories, important flint mines were first opened about 2500 BC. The

Green stone axes from Cornwall.

KILLIN

RATHLIN

TIEVEBULLIAGH

GT. LANGDALE

GRAIG LWYD

GRIMES GRs.

CORNDON

PEMBROKE

▲EASTON DOWN

CAMBOURNE

MOUNTS BAY

Some sites of stone-axe factories and flint mines.

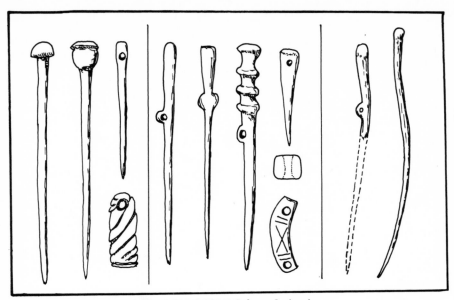

Bone pins and pendants of c.2,500-2,000 BC from Ireland,
Orkney, and southern England.

mines at Grimes Graves cover almost a hundred acres, and are more
sophisticated than those of Sussex. Here the miners dug their circular
shafts, but from the base of these shafts they dug a series of radial galleries which followed the seams of flint. They worked with antler picks
and aurochs shoulder-blade shovels, in these low galleries sometimes
lit by small oil-lamps carved from lumps of chalk. Waste material was
often left, together with broken picks, on the base of the shaft, whilst
in the areas around the shafts were working floors where the flint was
flaked. Although some of the flint tools used by the first farmers remained in use, there were one or two notable additions to the reper-
toire, of which the most significant were probably the wedge- or chisel-
shaped arrowhead and the polished-edge knife. At the same time the
craft of working bone and antler seems to have become more popular,
and its products indicate an increasing interest in self-adornment.
Long bone pins are found widely, if not in great quantities, in Southern Britian, and can be matched by more numerous examples from Ireland and the Isle of Man. Beads, pendants and tools were also made of
bone in these western regions, and the rich bone and antler finds of the

period just before 2000 BC in Orkney suggest that there too, between 2700-2200 BC, the working of bone had developed into a skilled craft. This does not necessarily mean that all the products of this craft were new inventions or that they must indicate a change in the nature or style of clothes which were worn. The long yew-wood pins recovered from the Sweet Track demonstrate that similar items were being made at least five hundred years before. Whether or not the adoption of bone jewellery reflects changing tastes or fashions is uncertain, but an increasing interest in decoration and display does seem evident in this period, from the carved slabs of the megalithic monuments down to the ordinary household pots and pans. The pottery used by the early farmers was gradually modified so that shapes changed and decoration became more important. At the same time the fabrics became generally coarser and thicker, and the rims of the pots heavier and more pronounced. The significance of these changes in the quality and fineness of the pottery is not clear, but it may be significant that in this period we have no evidence for the activities of specialised potteries like those of the Lizard and the Frome district in an earlier time.

Grooved ware bowls and storage jar.

56

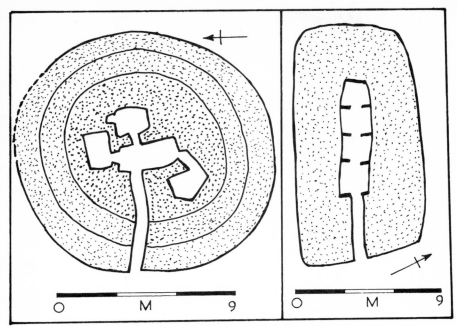

A chambered tomb on Wideford Hill, and a stalled cairn at Yarso, Orkney Is.

Whereas the pottery of the first farmers had been almost completely undecorated that of the period from 2700 to 2200 BC reveals an increasing tendency to cover the whole pot with decoration in some form or other. Much of this decoration was patternless, and consisted of all-over impressions made with a bone point, a finger-nail, or a length of twisted cord. One large group of pottery stands out from the rest in being deliberately patterned, and that is the pottery decorated with shallow grooves now known as "grooved ware". Some of the nicest pots of this kind are flat-bottomed dishes with straight sides, which have carefully arranged patterns of lines, zig-zags and lozenges around them. In contrast are a group of much coarser, bucket-like, vessels with simple grooved cross-hatching, but these pots with their possible imitation of basketry may point to the origins of this particular style.

The "grooved ware" is found on many sites in Southern and Eastern England but north of Yorkshire its only major concentration at present is in the Orkney Islands. Here, its main period of use may fall after

The interior of the passage grave at Fourknocks.

2200 BC, and it certainly continued in use after that date in England too. The pottery which preceded it in Orkney (called Unston ware) has been found inside a number of remarkable stone-built tombs of this period. Some of these, like that at Unston itself, are under round cairns and have either a series of small burial chambers opening off a central room, or else a series of 'stalls' formed by large flat slabs of stone projecting in pairs from the side walls of a single chamber or gallery. This arrangement was developed, particularly on the island of Rousay, into a tomb covered by a long mound and containing up to fourteen stalls, each of which seems to have been originally intended for one burial. The supreme example of Orcadian architecture of this period, however, is the great tomb of Maes Howe, where a circular cairn over a hundred feet in diameter and twenty-five feet high covers a central chamber with three side-vaults for burials. The whole tomb is built of fine slabs of unworked stone, expertly fitted, fronted in the angles by monolithic buttresses, and covered by a corbelled beehive vault. The care lavished on the building of Maes Howe suggests that it was intended for the burial of a powerful and respected chieftain, but we shall never know for certain since the tomb was later completely looted by Viking raiders to Orkney.

Maes Howe is generally thought to owe its inspiration to contemporary or slightly earlier megalithic tombs found in Ireland, particularly in the valley of the Boyne. At New Grange there is an extensive cemetery where about thirty tombs of various sizes are now known. The

59

Interior of Maes Howe tomb, Orkney.

The stone at the entrance to the tomb passage at New Grange.

cemetery is dominated by the great circular mounds of Knowth, Dowth and New Grange. Each of these covers one or two principal burial chambers, each set at the end of a great passage lined with massive orthostats. Around the edge of the covering mound at each tomb is a continuous kerb of large stones; at Knowth there were originally probably as many as a hundred and forty. Again, the sheer size of the tombs and the effort needed to build them suggests that they were the burial place of great chieftains, and that the many tombs at New Grange might represent a dynastic cemetery. The impression is enhanced by the cluster of small tombs which encircle the great tomb of Knowth, in much the same way as the mastabas of the Egyptian princes and nobility surround the pyramids of Giza. It is in the Boyne tombs, and just occasionally in those of Orkney and Anglesey, that we again meet with the passion for decoration and display. The kerb-stones, passages, and burial chambers of these tombs are all richly decorated with elaborate designs which were picked into their surface.

60

Carved stone balls from north-east Scotland.

At Knowth, for example, even preliminary examination of the tombs and kerb have revealed over a hundred and thirty decorated stones. The decoration is varied, including superb spirals, arcs, serpentiforms, lozenges, zig-zags, and 'wheel' or 'sun' motifs, several of which often appear together on a single stone. It is clear that the men who worked these stones did so with vigour, imagination, and a feel for composition and design; yet it is quite certain that the carvings were not executed for purely aesthetic reasons. Recent work at New Grange has shown that many carvings were either put on the rear surfaces of stones, or else in other positions where they would be covered when the tomb was completed. There is little doubt that the carvings had a magical or religious purpose and that they were not intended primarily for human eyes. Their real significance will probably never be understood.

The same must be said for a number of chalk or stone balls, about 3-4 inches in diameter, which have been found in some of the Boyne tombs. Others have been found in the Isle of Man and in Wessex, and far more numerous, decorated, examples have been discovered in Northern Scotland, where they carry spirals and other designs found on the slabs and stones of the Irish tombs. The lozenges and zig-zags, and indeed occasional spirals, found on "grooved ware" in both the far north and in Wessex also seem to point to a spread of the motifs and art style of the Boyne area towards the end of the period.

Apart from one or two tombs in the north-west corner of Wales, however, tombs of the Boyne type do not seem to have been adopted in the same way. The earlier megalithic tombs in the West Country, in South-West Scotland and in Northern Ireland frequently continued in use down to the end of the period if not beyond. Carbon dates for the final closing of tombs in Armagh and Antrim range from 2600 to about 1800 BC, whilst several Scottish tombs have impressed pottery or its contemporaries in their blocking material. The blocking-up of forecourts, and burial chambers seems to have been done with care and due ceremony, and sometimes was done with occupation debris apparently brought from a settlement in the area. In England at least, the gradual abandonment and closing of the long barrows and their megalithic chambers was paralleled by the gradual adoption of other forms of cemetery site. Round barrows begin to appear in Wessex, Yorkshire and Derbyshire, and, occasionally, in areas in between. Whether or not the adoption of this form of cairn was related to the influences emanating from the west and the north, where circular burial mounds were in use much earlier, we cannot say. On the other hand, some of these English round barrows now cover cremations and these were rare in the earlier period except perhaps in Eastern England, whereas they were normal in Ireland and common in South-West Scotland.

In fact the other type of cemetery which makes its appearance in Southern Britian at this time is the flat cremation cemetery. There were several such cemeteries closely grouped at Dorchester (Oxon) and the site of Stonehenge was the situation of another. The widespread adoption of this form of cemetery is attested by further examples in North Wales (Llandegai), Scotland (Cairnpapple), and the Isle of Man (Ballateare). Most of these cremations were not accompanied by grave-goods and those that were rarely yielded more than one or two pieces of flint-work, and the occasional bone pin. The most signifi-

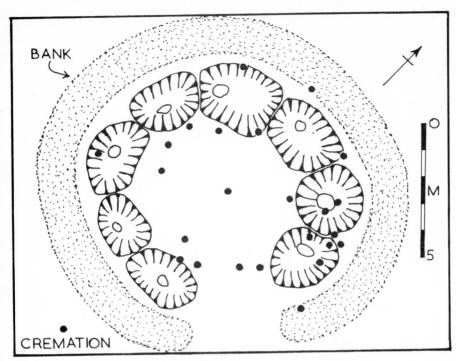

A henge monument at Dorchester, Oxon.

cant feature of these cemeteries is perhaps their location. Some, though not all, occur inside the banks and ditches of so-called henge monuments. At present the earliest such monument we know of, on the basis of carbon dating, is one at Llandegai dating to about 2,700 BC. This is followed by another at Arminghall (Norfolk) of about 2,600 BC. To these we may add, on the evidence of pottery, one or two of the small henges at Dorchester (Oxon) and another at Maxey (Northants). These henges, and others like them which cannot yet be dated, are much less spectacular than Stonehenge in its stone period, although the earliest henge monument at Stonehenge is itself C.14 dated to about 2,300 BC. This and the other early henges comprise a circular ditch and bank with a single entrance. Inside, or sometimes in the bottom of the ditch, there are often small pits which have been dug and then re-filled soon after. At Dorchester one of these pits was found in each segment of the ditch in three of the small henge monu-

63

ments, while at Stonehenge the famous Aubrey Holes are of this type. There, and elsewhere, it was sometimes these pits which subsequently had cremations inserted into them.

What the function of these henges was is still debated but the size of the later examples, which include the stone monuments of Stonehenge, and to some extent their distribution, argues that they were ceremonial centres erected by, and for, large populations which occupied territories covering hundreds of square miles. Most of these earlier henges are much smaller — often less than 200 feet in diameter — and may not have reached the same degree of importance but their basic function must have been much the same. If this were so, then they would have replaced the "causewayed camps" which seem to have fulfilled the function of tribal ceremonial centres at an earlier period. Whether or not there is any significance in the fact that some of the early henges have causewayed, as opposed to continuous, ditches remains to be proved. We now know that henges are also to be found in Ireland, and one group is centred in the same area as the New Grange cemetery. Earlier ritual sites in Ireland, such as Goodland and Lyles Hill, with their circular banks and internal pits might provide possible ancestors for the henge monument; certainly there are no similar structures known elsewhere in Europe and the henge monument can be safely indentified as a British invention. These further suggestions of contact, and an exchange of ideas, between Ireland and the mainland of Britain might lead us to one final speculation. Could the massive mound of Silbury Hill — over 550 feet in diameter and 130 feet high — have been inspired by the impressive cairns of New Grange, Knowth and Dowth? We now know that New Grange was built about 2,700 BC and Knowth possibly earlier; Silbury Hill is almost half a millennium younger.

2,200–1,700 BC

The construction of Silbury Hill, which perhaps required as much as twenty million man-hours from the builders, makes a convenient, as well as a prominent, monument to the end of one era and the beginning of another. A C. 14 date suggests that it was erected about 2300-2200 BC. Further carbon dates reveal that by the latter date new immigrants from the Continent of Europe were arriving in Britain in some numbers; the first immigrants to which archaeological evidence bears witness, since the first farmers some fifteen hundred years before. These new people, whom we recognise by their distinctive pottery "beakers", made several significant contributions to the development of prehistoric societies in Britain, the most obvious of which is the use of working of metals. The earliest of these new settlers are at present identified at New Grange and Ballnagilly in Ireland, where they were present by about 2200 BC. By 2000 BC they were certainly in Wessex and East Anglia, and the earliest dated examples from Yorkshire are only a little later. In fact, it seems likely that they occupied the South, East, and North-East of England, as well as parts of Ireland, within the space of a century or so. Whether this initial migration was followed by others is a point about which archaeologists still argue. The balance of the evidence suggests that after the first influx of settlers there were no further significant migrations, but that close contacts maintained with the Continent led to some changes in the shapes and decoration of the beakers themselves.

These immigrants, who for ignorance of their real name we call the Beaker people, had come here from the Rhineland and, on the whole, they seem to represent a new people as well as a new culture. They were of medium height, averaging about 5′ 6″ (men somewhat taller, women somewhat shorter), rather slender in build and with roundish heads on which the brow ridges were quite prominent. In general they seem to have been quite healthy people, capable of living to forty or fifty years of age and not suffering seriously from malnutrition, arthritis or dental disease. For many years there was no satisfactory evidence of where they lived. Many sites produced their pottery together with domestic refuse, pits and hearths, but no remains of substantial buildings could be found. For this reason, and the accumulating evidence from the rubbish deposits, the Beaker people were identified as nomadic pastoralists living in tents or other flimsy, temporary shelters. Some of the sites where no evidence of building could be found covered sizeable areas and contained many hearths and pits and would seem to be places which were occupied by several families. Such was the case at Lakenheath, and at New Grange where Beaker people settled around the foot of the great tomb.

Small farmsteads still seem to have been the normal form of settlement, however, and in recent years several such sites have been excavated in various parts of the country. Some of them appear to have had a single circular or oval hut, like those found at Gwithian (Cornwall) and Beacon Hill (Yorks) respectively, erected on a framework of timber posts or stakes. Other farmsteads, however, had pairs of huts, and these have been found at widely separated points such as Belle Tout (Sussex), Downpatrick (Co. Down), and Northton (Harris). Most of these huts, and others at Lough Gur, were either circular or oval with the exception of those at Belle Tout. Improvements over earlier huts are indicated by the porches which protect the entrances of the Downpatrick and Gwithian huts, but in size there is little difference. The two rectangular huts erected at Belle Tout were later replaced by three new huts, situated inside a ditched and banked enclosure. This is the earliest enclosed farmstead yet recognised in Britain, and skilful excavation of it has enabled us to say something about the way it was organised and how the economy operated. The enclosure at Belle Tout was trapezoidal and at its maximum measured about 360 by 240 feet. The second phase of occupation was found concentrated in the eastern end of this area, and it is possible that there were other hut complexes in the enclosure making up a small community rather than an individual farmstead. On the other hand, the major part of the enclosed space may have served as a cattle pound. Inside the eastern entrance were two huts, both probably used for domestic occupation, and each with three associated pits for storing grain. They probably shared the use of a large midden just to one side of the entrance, and although flint knapping sites, working areas and hearths were all

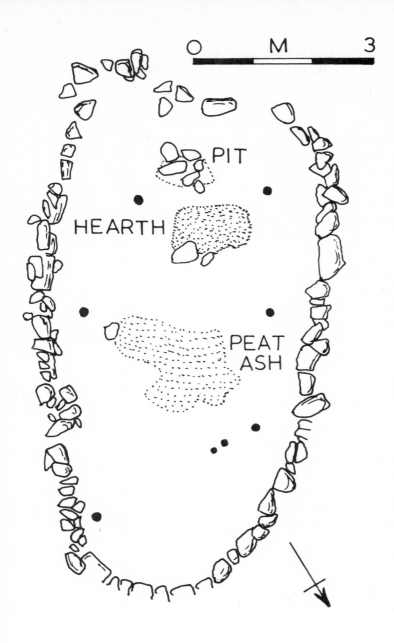

O　M　3

PIT

HEARTH

PEAT ASH

An oval Beaker house at Northton, Harris.

found so distributed that each hut could have had its own, the evidence suggests that the various working sites were each used for different purposes rather than by different households. In one area, a collection of heavy pounders and a store of calcined flint may indicate where the clay used for the rather coarse beakers found on the site was prepared for use. All these various features and structures may have been surrounded by a slight palisade, hedge or low bank which demarcated the main domestic area. Just outside this area was the third hut, oval in shape but probably open on one side and seemingly used as a flint working site.

Some indication that the rest of the enclosure was used as a cattle pound comes from the large quantity of scrapers, of several specialised types, which were found in the domestic compound. These would have been used largely in the preparation and working of hides and leather. At the same time, grain impressions, sickle flints and the surviving evidence of field weeds suggests that there were arable fields nearby in which emmer wheat and barley were grown. The mixed pastoral and arable economy which probably operated at Belle Tout is attested at other Beaker sites too, including Ballynagilly and Gwithian. At South Street the plough marks of the fourth millennium BC are matched by others made by Beaker farmers who also ploughed the fields in two directions at right angles to one another. Here, at Belle Tout and Ballynagilly, the evidence shows that the Beaker farmers were re-clearing and re-ploughing land which had reverted to grassland or even light woodland. The new farmers, however, showed a marked preference for barley, which might be related to the onset of drier and warmer conditions at about this time. Whether or not the combination of barley and beakers points to the production of beer is less certain. The decline in the importance of sheep, which began perhaps about the middle of the third millennium, seems to have continued, for, apart from the evidence from Belle Tout, the animal bones from Beaker rubbish deposits at Newgrange, Northton, Gorsey Bigbury (Somerset) and elsewhere consistently reveal the cow as by far the most important domesticate. At Northton it seems to have been the only domestic food animal, but at Gorsey Bigbury and Newgrange pig was also favoured, even in preference to sheep.

As we noted at Belle Tout, the increasing importance of cattle in the farming economy is reflected not only in the rubbish deposits containing animal bones but also in the quantity and variety of flint tools used in the preparation of hides. It is not surpising therefore that some of the flint mines continued to be worked in this period, including Grimes Graves and Easton. Indeed, at the latter it is Beaker pottery which is associated with traces of small huts which seem to have been occupied, perhaps seasonally, by the flint miners. Equally the stone axe factories continued in production, and although the Beakers cannot be proved to have acquired 'an interest' in them, several of the factories began to produce implements which are found in association with Beakers and were almost certainly introduced by them. These are the perforated stone heads commonly called battle-axes, which begin to appear in Beaker graves from about 2000 BC onwards. Early examples are made of rock from axe factories in Cornwall, North Wales and Pembrokeshire, and are thickly distributed in East Anglia and Yorkshire as well as being found, more thinly spread, over much of Southern and Eastern England and the East of Scotland. Whether these implements were really weapons is uncertain, but their comparatively blunt edges suggest they may not have been of much use for tree

A collection of barbed-and-tanged arrowheads found on the Cotswolds.

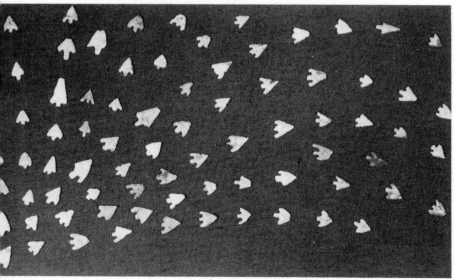

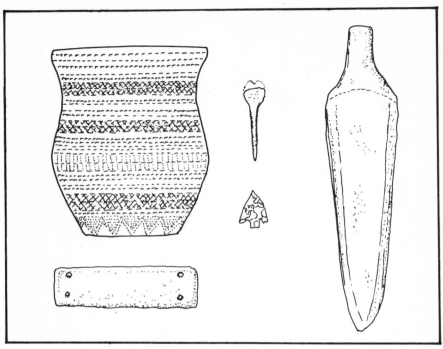

A Beaker grave-group from Roundway, Wilts.

felling or wood-working. At the same time there are other signs in the material belongings of the Beaker people that they were more warlike, or at least better equipped to defend themselves, than the indigenous population of Britain. A whole series of Beaker graves has produced a characteristic group of grave-goods which clearly belonged to archers. The most common finds are the barbed-and-tanged arrowheads themselves, but small bone wrist-guards to protect the wrist from the bowstring are not rare and there are several examples of grooved stones used for straightening arrows. Their bows are less frequently preserved but they are known to have used a slender long bow, and it has been suggested that they also had the use of an improved composite bow, shorter and stouter with well-defined nocks and transverse strapping of leather thongs. The armoury of the Beaker people was completed by a variety of copper and bronze daggers, which were mainly either riveted to their haft or held in it by a long tang. Some of the daggers are very short, with only two or three inches projecting from the

70

haft and their value as offensive weapons may have been limited. It seems likely that these daggers were in fact all-purpose knives, but in any case they represented a great advance over the flint knife and many of them show signs of wear and use accumulated over a long period of time. Apart from daggers the Beaker metalworker also produced other tools, such as the flat axe and the awl, and items of jewellery such as 'basket' earrings and pins. Many of these items were made of copper or arsenical bronze but some which have been analysed reveal the use of a good tin-bronze. An awl of tin-bronze found in a grave on Overton Down (Wilts) is associated with a carbon date which places it about 2150 BC, and the early appearance of Beaker people in Ireland may be related to the exploitation of Irish sources of tin and copper.

Ireland also produced gold, and the Beaker people seem to have been expert workers in this medium too. Occasional pieces of Beaker gold jewellery in the form of discs and earrings, and possible Beaker products such as the gold boat model from Broighter, are outnumbered by the superb gold *lunulae* (crescentic neckpieces) found mainly in Ireland. A recent study of these shows that most of the eighty examples known from Ireland were decorated with motifs found also on

Detail of the decoration on a gold *lunulae* from Ireland.

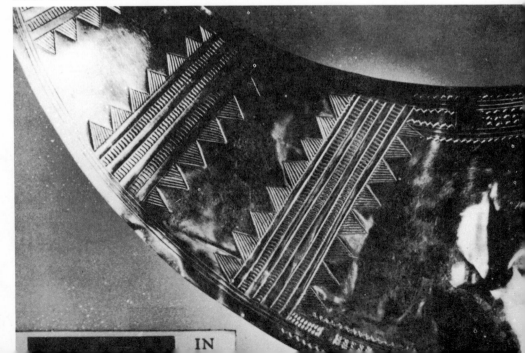

IN

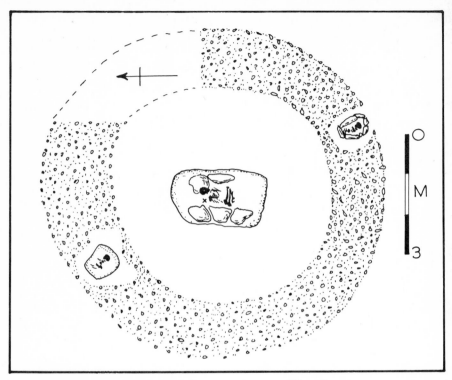

The primary Beaker burials under a round barrow at West Overton.

Beaker pottery, and there can be little doubt that Beaker goldsmiths were responsible for making most of the gold *lunulae* which are known. It seems equally certain that the men who made these *lunulae* were specialist goldsmiths, and it may be that there was a general trend towards specialisation of labour amongst the Beaker people in Britain. Whether or not the archer's equipment found in many Beaker graves points to the existence of specialist archers is uncertain, but the extraction and working of copper and tin seems likely to have been a specialist occupation, though not necessarily a full time one. There is accumulating evidence, too, of the appearance of specialist leatherworkers. A number of Beaker graves have produced groups of objects which seem to comprise leatherworkers' tool kits, the best example being the burial at the centre of Overton. Here, a man of forty years of age or more was buried with a beaker and a group of eight objects.

One of the henges at Knowlton, Dorset.

These included a bronze awl, two slate rubbers, an antler softener, a flint knife, and a firelighting kit (a flint strike-a-light and ball of marcasite) which could have been used in the smoke-curing of skins.

Alongside these various craftsmen, Beaker society may have supported one further group of specialists who produced no manufactured goods but were nevertheless considered indispensable members of the community — the priests, seers or soothsayers, whichever term one thinks most applicable. In a sense we have no direct evidence of these men; we have no drawings or paintings of them, no

73

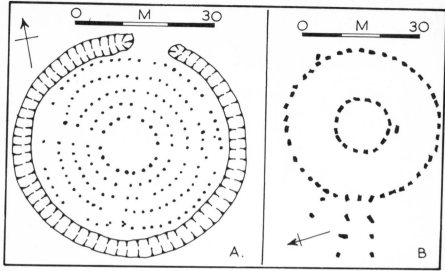

A. timber 'temple' inside the henge at Mt. Pleasant and B. the Stone Circles in the Sanctuary, Overton.

regalia which we can identify as theirs, and no priestly burials with associated cult objects. But we do have the 'temples' in which they officiated, and in the design of the 'temples' we can identify their long and careful observation of solar and lunar phenomena. The Beaker peoples' 'temples' were, in fact, henge monuments which we have earlier seen as the invention of the peoples occupying Britain in the first half of the third millennium BC. Why the Beaker people should have adopted, and then modified, this type of monument for their own use cannot be determined, but they are clearly associated with many of the larger and later henges.

It is generally supposed that they were responsible for the development of the henges with two or four entrances, and a more ovoid shape than the one-entrance, circular henges erected earlier. Recent excavations at some of the biggest of these henges — Durrington Walls, Marden and Mount Pleasant — have shown that here the main earthworks were built by people who used 'grooved ware' and that the Beakers only became involved in the later use of these henges. At Mount Pleasant their involvement is marked by the replacement of a large circular timber building, inside the enclosure, with a setting of upright sarsen monoliths arranged around three sides of a square. The associa-

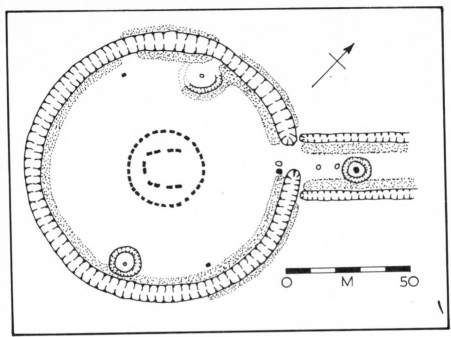

Stonehenge as it was c. 1,800-1,700 BC.

tion between Beakers and the erection of stone circles or settings inside henges is repeated elsewhere. At Avebury, where the enclosing bank covered impressed and grooved pottery, beakers were found in some of the sockets dug for the hundred or so stones of the outer circle. Further beakers were found with dedicatory burials at the foot of two of the two hundred stones forming the West Kennet Avenue which leads from Avebury to a much smaller monument, the Sanctuary, on Overton Hill. Here too, a circular timber hut was demolished and replaced by two concentric stone circles; a dedicatory burial here also contained a beaker. Stonehenge itself repeats the story. Inside the earlier henge, perhaps about 1800 BC, a double-circle of holes was dug to take about eighty uprights of bluestone, brought from the Prescelly mountains of Pembrokeshire.

At the same time a "processional way" or avenue was constructed, as at Avebury, but here flanked by bank and ditch rather than pairs of stones. In the event, the bluestone circles were not completed, and instead a circle of thirty massive sarsens joined by sarsen lintels was erected, and inside these, five sarsen trilithons, of even greater size. Most of these stones are still visible at Stonehenge.

The addition of stone circles and settings to the henge monuments represents the use of new skills, particularly to overcome the problem of transporting large stones over considerable distances. The Prescelly bluestones were probably brought by raft along the south coast of Wales, and thence by river to within two miles of Stonehenge. Sarsens could be found much nearer, on the Marlborough Downs twenty miles to the north, but the problems they represented were much greater because of their enormous size and weight. The biggest of them weighed fifty tons! We can never know how these huge stones were moved from the Downs to Stonehenge, but it seems likely that a combination of sledges or cradles and innumerable wooden rollers were used. Once at the henge itself, they had to be erected, and here a knowledge of levers must have been employed. In addition to the use of these skills, the sarsens at Stonehenge were worked and shaped. The lintels, for example, were worked to form a true circle above the uprights, and they were fixed to the uprights by mortice and tenon joints! All in all the creation of Stonehenge represents a remarkable organisation of skill and manpower, amounting perhaps to as much as thirty million man-hours!

The exact contribution made by the Beaker people in the building of Stonehenge and the development of the other henge monuments is still not clear. Henge monuments themselves were certainly in existence long before the Beaker people arrived in Britain, and even some of the large henges with two and four entrances seem to have been built without Beaker involvement. Similarly, there is no reason to think that the Beaker people introduced stone circles and settings into Britain. Two recent carbon dates have dated the Ring of Stenness in Orkney to the middle of the third millennium BC, a stone circle in Tyrone to about 2300 BC, and a stone setting at Duntreath (Stirling) to before 3000 BC. At the same time we have a timber circle at Croft Moraig (Perthshire) associated with the pottery of the early farmers. The Beaker contribution would therefore seem to be restricted to the bringing together of the two separate traditions — stone settings and henges — except in the case of Stonehenge where many apparently new skills are displayed.

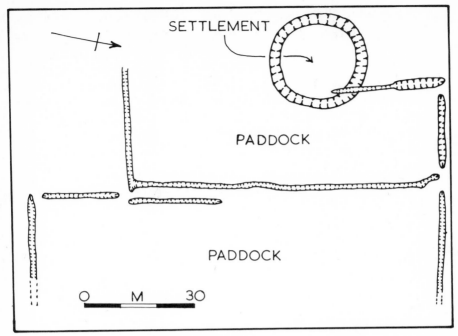

A farming settlement of about 2,000 BC at Fengate.

The adoption of the henge monument by the Beaker people strongly suggests some degree of mixing, if not fusion, between them, and the indigenous population. It is quite clear that when the Beaker people arrived in Britain they did not slaughter or drive out the existing occupants, and that these people survived as recognisable communities throughout the period. According to carbon dates, it was not until about 2100 BC that some of their largest and most impressive monuments were built. Of these the henge of Durrington Walls is the most outstanding. It is the biggest henge in Britain, 1600 feet in diameter, surrounded by a bank a hundred feet wide, and a ditch fifty feet wide and twenty feet deep! All this was dug with the usual antler picks and shoulder-blade shovels. Inside Durrington there were at least two timber circles, probably buildings, and these are matched by others found at Marden, Mount Pleasant and Woodhenge. One supposes that such buildings were 'temples', probably open to the sky at the centre, but they may well have served also as meeting places for tribal gatherings.

77

The village of Skara Brae, Orkney, c.2,000 BC.

The ordinary lives of these people seem to have gone on much the same as before the arrival of the Beaker people, the erection of ever bigger henge temples, and the introduction of metalworking. They occasionally acquired items of copper or bronze, like the axe found in the ditch at Mount Pleasant, but their pottery and their flint tools reveal little or no change. On the other hand they had no more control over their life than the Beaker people, and we see similar changes taking place in their farming economy to those noted from Beaker settlements. Cattle and pig assume more importance as the role of the sheep declines, and barley increases in use at the expense of wheat. A farmstead site recently excavated at Fengate, and carbon dated to about 2100-2000 BC, revealed these trends very clearly both in the animal bone samples (where only seven per cent were sheep) and in the surroundings of the farm. Although no huts were found, they were almost certainly situated in a ditched, circular enclosure about sixty-five feet in diameter. Just beyond this was an area used for flint-working and this stood in one of at least two, and probably more ditch-enclosed paddocks. These were rectangular, about three hundred feet long and a third as wide, with entrances in each corner and probably with drove-ways between them. Together with the evidence of the animal bones, these paddocks suggest we are looking at the remains of a farm where cattle-rearing was the most important activity.

The same trends can be observed in the far north in the villages of Skara Brae and Rinyo in Orkney. Recent carbon dates place Skara Brae at the very beginning of this period rather than in the preceding one as was once thought. Here we have an undoubted village of seven or eight separate households, built in a huddled group to protect them from the Atlantic storms. With plenty of large flat slabs with which to build, the 'grooved ware' makers who occupied the village were able to erect very comfortable homes for themselves which, because they were of stone and were subsequently covered by sand, have survived almost intact to the present day.

Each house was roughly square with rounded corners and comprised basically one large room, off which one or two small chambers opened. The walls rose to about eight feet in height and the roof was probably made of skins or turf supported on whalebone, or just possibly wooden rafters. Each house had a square fireplace at its centre, and rectangular 'boxes' of stone built against the walls on two sides. These were the beds, originally packed with heather, and covered by canopies, the stone supports of which survive in some of the houses. Flat stones were used as seats and working tables, and most of the huts also sported fine stone-built dressing tables, while personal belongings could be stored inside small cubby-holes built into the wall over the beds. In one corner of each house there were rectangular cists built of slabs set edgeways, and carefully luted with clay to make them water-tight. They may have served as tanks in which shell-fish could be kept fresh until they were to be eaten. Shell-fish and other sea-food certainly formed an important part of the diet of the Skara Brae population, but cattle and barley were no doubt the basic elements.

This village overlaid the remains of similar but generally smaller houses, and the identical village at Rinyo was also found to be erected over earlier houses, from some of which Unstan as well as grooved pottery was found. Together with a stone-built house on Papa Westray, recently carbon dated to about 3000-2700 BC, these finds suggest that the tradition represented at Skara Brae goes back well before the arrival of the Beakers in either England or Ireland. But they eventually arrived even here, and a beaker was found in the latest period of occupation at Rinyo. In a situation where there was still plenty of land for all, and the rate of progress and speed of communication was relatively slow, it was almost inevitable that eventually the Beaker immigrants and the existing farmers should mix and integrate. To some extent we have already seen this process taking place in the henge monuments, and it is to be seen in other areas of activity too. For many years it was thought that Beaker burials were, almost universally, single inhumations which in Southern Britain were placed under round barrows and in Northern Britain (broadly, north of the Tees) were situated in cists. We now know that many Beaker burials were multiple and that cremations were not uncommon, particularly in Yorkshire and eastern England where the tradition of cremation was well established before the Beakers arrived. Here we seem to have evidence of the burial rites which the Beakers brought with them from the Rhineland being modified under the influence of local burial customs. On the other hand, some of the inhumation burials associated with impressed or grooved pottery and found under round barrows may belong to this rather than an earlier period and reflect the absorption of Beaker rites by the indigenous population. Whatever the truth concerning these burials, there can be no doubt that from about 2000 BC there was a gradual mixing and integration of the Beaker and non Beaker population in Britain. At the same time there was also the continuous development and evolution of existing societies under the influence of the newcomers. These two processes were responsible for the appearance, in the two centuries between 1800 and 1600 BC, of communities and peoples whose material belongings were neither those of the earlier farmers nor those of the Beaker settlers, but were something quite distinctive and new.

1,700–1,300 BC

In the period before the arrival of the people making Beaker pottery, we saw that there was a trend towards greater regional diversity in both the material belongings and the farming economy of the existing population. The results of interaction with the Beaker peoples and their way of life therefore varied from one region to another, and in particular from the Lowland zone of Britain (the area south and east of a line from the mouth of the Severn to the Humber) to the Highland zone. In the period between about 1700 and 1300 BC, the regional differences are to be seen in metalwork, jewellery, bonework, and pottery, as well as in ritual monuments. In Southern and Eastern Britain the onset of the new period is marked by the appearance of tall, flat-based pottery vessels with decorated collars, normally used as urns for the ashes of cremated bodies but also used as storage vessels on domestic occupation sites. This pottery has been shown to be a development from the latest of the impressed pottery wares, which were in use in England alongside the Beaker pottery.

Beaker influence itself can be detected in the shape of the foot used on many of these vessels, and sometimes in their decoration. As one might expect, the earliest appearances of these 'collared urns' are in Southern and Eastern England, where they appear from some time before 1700 BC onwards. Later they are found further North and West, although they were always most popular in the areas in which they first developed. Fragments of these collared urns have been found inside settlement sites at Shearplace Hill (Dorset) and Rams Hill (Berkshire), and the carbon dates from both sites would allow their foundation to be placed sometime just before 1300 BC.

The earliest settlement, at Shearplace Hill, consisted of an elongated, ditched enclosure containing probably a single round timber hut, Rams Hill was larger, possibly up to two and a half acres, and was enclosed by a ditch and bank, but it, too, was elongated, and may originally have had but a single timber hut of circular plan. A third site of

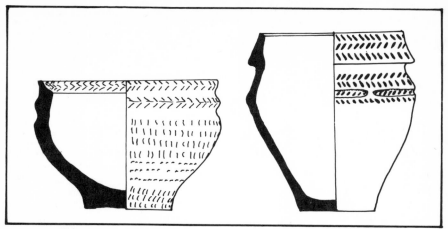

A 'Food Vessel' and a 'Collared Urn'.

broadly similar type but with two circular huts was recorded at Broom-wood in Kent and produced flintwork which could belong to this period. The earliest pottery from a fourth settlement, at Trevisker in Cornwall, came from vessels related to the collared urns and a lengthy occupation of the two huts here may have ended about 1200 BC, according to a carbon date. The two timber huts at Trevisker stood adjacent to one another and were both large enough (24 - 26 feet in diameter) to have been occupied as houses, although in one of the huts an upright loom had probably been erected as well. Unlike the huts from Wessex, these huts had two concentric rings of upright wooden posts which supported the walls and the roof rafters, and the walls themselves were strengthened by, if not actually built around, a series of stakes. The presence of a loom, from which some loomweights sur-vived, suggests that wool production may have played a role in the farming economy of the Trevisker settlement and there was probably sufficient rough grazing nearby to maintain sheep for this purpose. On the other hand the presence of several milling quernstones pointed to the production of grain, which here and elsewhere in Britain was by now mostly barley. In Wessex we might expect a similar mixed econ-omy to operate, but with cattle replacing sheep as the dominant domes-ticates. At Rams Hill cattle certainly played an important role in the later economy of the site but to what extent this is true of the first settle-ment here is uncertain. On present evidence it seems likely that there

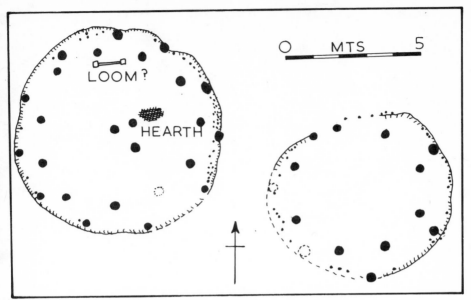

Timber huts at Trevisker, Cornwall, c.1,300 BC.

was an increasing trend towards pastoralism in this period, and that all of the excavated settlements—which seem to stand at the end of it—might be associated with a pastoral economy. An indication of the earlier importance of grain production might be found, however, in the small squarish 'Celtic' fields which in some cases are overlain or cut through by large linear ditches thought to be 'ranch' boundaries of the succeeding period.

The settlement at Trevisker may have been involved in other activities as well as farming, for tin-bearing pebbles were found both inside and outside the houses. With the increasing use of tin-bronze, Cornish tin would have become an important trade commodity. Hoards of metalwork suggest that bronzesmiths were itinerants rather than residents who worked for a single community. If settlements like Trevisker, Shearplace Hill and Rams Hill were typical of earlier and as yet unlocated settlements in southern Britain, then there were indeed no communities large enough to have supported resident bronzesmiths. Yet there can be little doubt that the bronzework used in this period was made by specialists. The use of tin to make bronze was carefully regulated, and two-part, closed moulds were employed, thus allowing

A small hoard of tools from Westbury-on-Trym, Avon, c.1,800-1,600 BC.

the production of more sophisticated artefacts. Personal weaponry was improved by the production of daggers with a thickened mid-section and a more pointed tip; grooves which followed the shape of the blade may have been functional, but were also decorative and sometimes outlined areas of pin-prick ('*pointille*') decoration down the centre of the blade. Metal spearheads also appear for the first time, and their variety—with tangs, sockets, collars and loops variously employed to ensure firm hafting to their shafts—testify to a bronze industry which was both experimental and inventive. There was increasing use of bronze for tools, and the flat axe was given flanges to hold it firmer in its haft and a more flaring blade to increase its effectiveness. The carpenter also benefited from the introduction of bronze chisels.

Apart from the appearance of several wooden coffins, there is not a great deal to testify to the continued development of carpentry in pre-historic Britain at this time, except for three boats found on the edge of the Humber at North Ferriby. But these three vessels, found within a hundred yards of one another, suggest that the skills of the boat builders at least were still increasing. Carbon dates suggest that the boats were built and used sometime within the period from about 1650 to 1300 BC. All three were probably about 45 feet long originally, made from oak planks which were sewn together, using yew stitches passed

A grave-group from Camerton, Soms.

through neat rows of holes bored along the edges of the planks. A contemporary bow of yew found at Edington Burtle (Soms) shows that, in contrast, the traditional craft of bow-making had changed little over the preceding millennium and a half. Whereas the carpenter and his craft were no doubt stimulated by the new tools which bronzesmiths were now making for them, the flint and stone industries must have faced increasing competition from the metalworkers.

Stone axes appear less frequently now, and often in a ritual rather than a domestic or industrial context. The latest carbon dates from Grime Graves point to the abandonment of the flint mines there some time around 1500 - 1400 BC, and after this period flint tools become increasingly fewer in number. For a time, however, the need for fine flint arrowheads continued and was met by the production of further barbed-and-tanged examples, including a variety with sharp straight

85

The barrow cemetery at Normanton, Wilts.

edges and broad barbs. Equally, the polished stone industry found continuing demand for battle-axes, and scope for new products such as maceheads and small perforated whetstones. The latter were possibly, and the former certainly, of some ceremonial importance. In Southern Britain, in this period, ceremony may have been centred mainly on funerary sites rather than other ritual monuments. Most of the henge monuments show few signs of activity after about 1700 BC, except for Mount Pleasant and some of the smallest henges such as City Farm (Oxon) and Fargo Plantation (Wilts). Stonehenge, of course, is an exception to which we must return shortly, but its continued importance is revealed by the incredible concentration of burial mounds of this period in the area immediately around it. It has been estimated that there are surviving records or traces of over four thousand round barrows of about this period in Wessex as a whole, but nowhere do they cluster more thickly than around Stonehenge. These barrows take a variety of forms, some of which are almost or entirely exclusive to Wessex. They are found in close-set groups which seem to represent the cemeteries of individual tribes or clans, and which are sometimes strung out in a neat line. Where excavations have been carried out, the focus of the cemetery—the founder's grave if you like—has often been found to be a Beaker burial. This would seem to imply that in the fusion of native and immigrant peoples and traditions in the period before 1700 BC, it was the immigrant Beaker people who took the more prominent role. The widespread adoption of the round barrow, and the practice of burying the deceased with equipment such as bronze daggers, bone or bronze pins, battle-axes and arrowheads, also points to the continuing strength of Beaker traditions. Whether or not the erection of stake-circles like those at Arreton Down (IoW) and Bishop Cannings (Wilts), and the use of coffins in barrow burials at Winterbourne Stoke (Wilts), Latch Farm (Dorset) and elsewhere, also represents the maintenance of Beaker traditions, is not quite so certain, but seems likely. On the other hand earlier, non-Beaker, funerary rites also persist and are often found associated, in the same barrows, with these Beaker traits. Most notable is the increasing importance of cremation, in which the collared urns obviously play an important part, and the frequency of multiple burials. It is only recently that archaeologists have begun to recognise that many Wessex barrows covered not one but several burials, and that more than one of these burials were made before the barrow itself was erected.

These burial rites are very similar indeed to those found in Yorkshire, sometimes associated with the collared urns but more frequently with a different type of flat-bottomed storage jar commonly called a 'food vessel' by archaeologists. Food vessels, like collared urns, seem to have a mixed ancestry in which the importance of the Beaker element varies from one region to another. In Ireland the food vessel bowls seem to have a very close relationship with the Beakers, whereas in Yorkshire the connection is more distant and less pronounced. On present evidence it seems likely that the food vessels developed as a distinctive type of pottery somewhat earlier than the collared urns, for more than a dozen sites have produced these pots in situations which can be shown to be earlier than collared urns on the same site. The appearance of food vessels in Southern Britain, however, is in general relatively late; their primary area of use seems to have been in the North and in Ireland. Here, even more than in Southern Britain perhaps, there is little evidence for the settlements which were occupied in this period, so much so that for many years the makers of food vessels have been described as either migrant traders or nomadic pastoralists. It is, in fact, possible that these people had advanced further towards the establishment of large communities than their contemporaries in Southern Britain. On the promontory of Mullaghfarna (Co. Sligo) about fifty stone-built enclosures between 20 and 40 feet in diameter represent the hut-sites of a large community which lived there at some date almost certainly before about 1000 BC. Unfortunately no artefacts have been recovered from this village to date it more precisely, and the same applies to a smaller but similar settlement discovered (from the air) at Knocknashee in the same county. The story is repeated at Danby Ring in Yorkshire where fifty acres of the spur of a hill are enclosed by a double stone wall, presumably built to defend a settlement. The erection of a stone circle and a cemetery of round cairns just outside the defences suggest that the wall, and the presumed settlement, may belong to this period, but at present there is no evidence to confirm this. That these people were, to some extent at least, a sedentary population is suggested by evidence both from Ireland (e.g. Ballynagilly) and England (East Derbyshire) where they were responsible for the introduction and extension of pastureland. In the absence of domestic occupation sites, and the rubbish which accumulates on them, it is difficult for us to be sure what particular form the pastoral economy took, but the rarity of any wool-working equipment and the evidence from Southern Britain suggests that cattle used most of the available grassland. We should not, however, think in terms of highland communities made up of pastoralists alone. As in Southern Britain, so in the North and in Ireland there were distinctive 'schools' of metalworking which emerge in this period. In Scotland and the North of England, several hoards of bronzework like that from Migdale, suggest that as in Southern England, bronzesmiths were itinerants at this time. This is confirmed by the scattered distribution of the open stone moulds used to cast the flat axes, rings, and bar-ingots produced by the Northern metalworkers. From the bar ignots they were able to beat rings, tubular beads, and bangles, and the production of sheet copper or bronze jewellery is one notable feature of the industry.

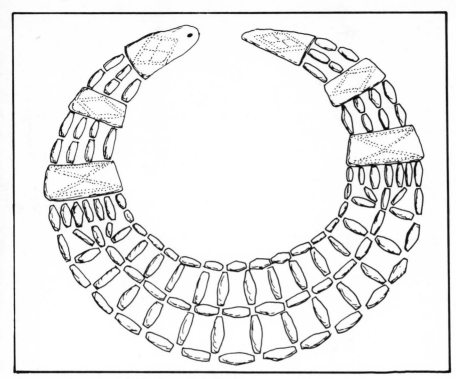

A crescentic necklace of jet from Poltallock.

Irish smiths developed their own industries, in which flat axes and halberds played an important part, and by the middle of the second millennium BC were producing their own varieties of the flanged axe, the socketed spearhead and the grooved dagger.

Locally produced grooved daggers also appear in some Scottish burials of this period, and these include examples with gold pommel mounts. Three such gold mounts, together with some gold discs from Orkney and some rather crudely decorated *lunulae* from Scotland may represent a Scottish gold-working industry related to, but intermediate between, those of the Beaker people in Ireland and of Wessex towards the close of the period. Two *lunulae* of this group have been found further south, in north Wales and in Cornwall, and five more examples come from the Continent. These raise the possibility that the people who made and used food vessels in the North traded

A tomb at Clava, Inverness, with one of a surrounding circle of standing stones.

their goldwork in Western Britain and North-West Europe. They may also have been responsible for the export of the ten or so 'Irish' axes which have been found abroad, as well as others which reached Southern Britain in greater numbers. Their contacts with Europe are reflected in some of their own metalwork, such as the bronze armlets, which copy types produced in the Rhineland, and in the appearance both in Northern and Southern Britain of European types of metal pins. It is possible that a number of metal objects of Mediterranean origin also arrived here at this time. These include a fragment of a Mycenaean short-sword from Pelynt (Cornwall) and two double-axes from Topsham and Whitby. Indirect contacts with the Mediterranean may have been established either through the Rhineland and central Europe, or through Brittany and France. Mediterranean bronzes have also been found in Brittany and further south in France, and certainly there were close links between Brittany and Wessex in this period. Apart from metalwork, raw amber may have been brought into Bri-

The interior of the Clava tomb at Corriemony.

tain, from the Baltic, since this material became increasingly popular for jewellery. The food vessel users in Northern Britain tended to use jet from Yorkshire for their buttons and disc beads and for their decorated crescentic necklaces, but in Southern Britain amber was often used for these items instead.

Gold, amber, jet, bronze, stone, flint and bone—all these materials were used and apparently treasured by the users of food vessels, and where they occur together in graves they seem to indicate the burial of people of some importance. At Masterton (Fife), for example, the body lay with a bronze dagger, a bronze blade, a pair of armlets, a jet necklace and a hide. Under the great barrow at Towthorpe (Yorkshire), the burial relics included a bronze dagger, a stone macehead and a flint knife. These burials, and others with their gold-pommelled daggers, parallel the rich graves found in Wessex in the period from about 1400 BC to 1300 BC.

The general run of burials made with food vessels are indeed similar

The Rollright Stones, a stone circle in Oxfordshire.

A decorated cist slab from Poole Farm, Soms.

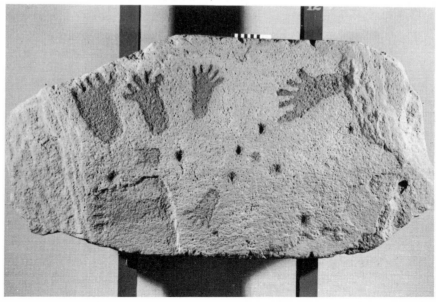

in many respects to those made with urns. They often occur in cemeteries, and though those in Scotland are mainly cemeteries of flat graves, further south in Yorkshire and Derbyshire round barrows are commonly used to cover the graves. As with urn burials, those with food vessels include both single and multiple examples and both cremations and inhumations. Sometimes, as at Bishops Waltham, a cremation and an inhumation are placed together. At Bishops Waltham there was also a wooden coffin, and about a dozen examples are now known from food vessel graves, including three found with other burials under a barrow at Dalgety in Fife.

These similarities to burials made with collared urns extend also to the appearance of stake-circles beneath some barrows containing food vessels, but other such barrows overlie a ring, not of stakes, but of stone. One is tempted to think that the stone rings and stake-circles were simply alternative versions of the same funerary enclosure, but at Tregullund (Cornwall), for example, both structures are found under the one barrow. Apart from these rings of stone buried under the barrow, other barrows with food vessels are associated with circles of standing stones. These may be free-standing circles of monoliths, as at Farway Down (Devon), or with monoliths set onto or into an earth or stone bank, as occurs at Druids Circle (Caernarvon) or Weird Law (Peebles). Burials made at the centre of the latter are carbon dated to about 1600 BC. Further north in Scotland there are more stone circles, each focussing on one great recumbent stone, which also have burials of this period at their centre, made inside a circular court surrounded by a cairn or stone bank. These monuments seem closely related to the Clava tombs around Inverness where fine stone circles stand around circular cairns with a passage which leads into a central burial chamber. At the Clava tombs, at stone circles elsewhere in Scotland, at the Tregullund barrow, and on the stones and slabs of other graves with food vessels, stones bearing artificially made cup-shaped depressions have been recorded. Their meaning has been much debated but no one has yet solved the mystery of why they were made. They are the most prolific carvings of a 'school' of rock-art which seems to be associated with the users of food vessels. Apart from the many cup-marks, there are smaller numbers of carvings of axes, feet, hands, and daggers from the lids or kerbs of cists and barrows containing burials with food vessels. These are found mainly in Scotland but also appear as far south

A gold lozenge from the Clandon Barrow, Dorset.

as the Badbury barrow (Dorset). The highland distribution of both the carvings and the various forms of stone circle is, of course, to be expected since it was only in these regions that the raw materials for stone circles and the working surfaces for rock-art could easily be acquired. But we saw in the previous chapter that the Beaker people were able to erect stone circles or other monuments inside the henges at Avebury, Stonehenge, and Mount Pleasant in Wessex. Similarly, rare examples of simple stone circles can be found in Wessex, such as the Rollright Stones (Oxon). More interesting perhaps is the appearance also of stone carvings, of axes, daggers, and feet, at a handful of sites in Wessex. The Badbury kerb stone was briefly mentioned above; quite different is the cist slab from Poole Farm (Soms) carved with feet and cup-marks, in addition to a curious horned object. The best known Wessex carvings, however, are those at Stonehenge, most of which are axes but also including daggers and a variety of other less specific shapes.

To some extent the various points of similarity which we have noticed between the people of the highland zone and those of Southern Britain may be explained by their similar ancestries—in the mixing of indigenous and Beaker traditions. On the other hand the increasing number of food vessels found in Southern England sug-

The gold breastplate from Bush Barrow, Wilts.

gests that perhaps the makers of these vessels themselves migrated south. This might help to explain the appearance of rock-carvings of a type normally found only in the highland zone at Stonehenge, Badbury and Poole Farm. Equally it might be associated with the apparently short-lived period of unusually wealthy burials found in Wessex, East Anglia and the South-West peninsula.

These burials are divided almost evenly between cremations and inhumations, and are accompanied by objects of fine craftsmanship and valuable, imported materials. Of these, the goldwork is the most eye-catching, consisting of decorative rectangular or lozenge-shaped plates, button and bead covers, discs, gold-pin decorated pommels, a pommel cover, a handled cup and objects of amber and other materials bound in gold sheet. Amber is itself a common material in these graves, used for beads and pendants, crescentic necklaces, handled cups, dagger pommels, and gold-bound discs and pendant handles.

Bronzework comprises mainly daggers and awls, but apart from some miniature cups pottery is scarce and only three graves have produced urns. The overall impression from these graves and their contents is that of an elite, able to accumulate wealth in the form of ostentatious display items. These various pieces together suggest a fashion for ornate jewellery, things in miniature (cups, 'halberd' pendants, 'battle-axe' beads), and composite artefacts made of two or more different materials. In the grave at Wilsford, for example, gold was found combined with shale, bone, bronze and amber. The fashion which these things, and indeed the rich burials as such, represent was probably short-lived. Apart from the fact that it was a fashion, rather than a continuous tradition, detailed study of the gold-work has suggested that much of it was made by only one or two craftsmen, and therefore probably within a period of not more than fifty or sixty years. The same study has also revealed some of the techniques and traits which characterise the goldwork from these rich burials, and might suggest where the origin of the fashion lay. The two most distinctive traits, perhaps, are the multiple linear borders and the dot-in-line pattern, both of which are foreshadowed in the *lunulae* of Scotland, which we have suggested were made by the users of food vessels. Whether or not the pin-prick decoration of Wessex daggers and minature cups might have been inspired by the very similar pin-prick patterns employed on the jet necklaces of Northern Britain is uncertain, but possible. In any case, it seems that there are several grounds for thinking that some of the users of food vessels did migrate southwards in the later part of the period and establish themselves in Wessex. They need not have done so by force. Recent studies have shown that by about 1500 BC the Wessex landscape was beginning to change, with arable giving way to pastureland as the warm dryish weather persisted. If, as we have supposed, the users of food vessels were a pastoralist population then their migration southwards and their subsequent rise to pre-eminence might be related to the changing environment. But whether or not it was men such as the chieftain buried under Bush Barrow—with his gold finery, his daggers and axe, and his ceremonial mace—who ordered the ranch boundaries to be laid across the arable fields only further research will reveal. At present, the little evidence available suggests that such drastic changes may only have come a century or two later.

CHAPTER SIX | 1,300 – 650 BC

The beginning of a new era, about 1300 BC, is marked partly by the passing of earlier fashions in burial, ritual, personal ornament and equipment, and partly by the adoption of new ones. These changes of fashion, however, do not seem to reflect any fundamental change in the basic pattern of life at this time. The farming economy seems largely unchanged, the settlement pattern remains much the same as in the preceding period, and there is no reason to think that there were any significant developments in the social organisation of the population. These things only began to alter after the hot, dry climate of the second millennium BC gradually began to give way to wetter, and eventually colder, weather after about 1000 BC or a little earlier. This brought about changes not only in farming but also in settlement and society, and paved the way for the tribal chiefdoms and hill-forts of the last seven centuries before Christ.

It is important to emphasise, however, that these changes took place only slowly, and that at the beginning of the period in particular, we are concerned as much with continuity as we are with change. This is true even of burial rites, which are often thought to be the most pronounced evidence of change at this time. In Southern England, certainly, the most distinctive and common burial site of this period is the flat cemetery of cremations in urns, which clearly represents a change from the mixture of inhumations and cremations under round barrows which were the norm in the preceding period. The change is underlined by the reluctance of the mourners to place grave-goods with the burials—a dramatic contrast to the wealth of personal equipment often left with burials in the eighteenth to fourteenth centuries BC. Equally the urns now used to carry cremated bones are different from the collared urns and their relatives used earlier. Some are well-made, globular vessels with a certain amount of decoration on their shoulders, others are roughly-made bucket-shaped pots with no more than a simple cordon of clay around the body for decoration.

Two urns from the Deverel cremation cemetery.

The origins of these urn types are still obscure, but although the globular ones might be related to similar types known in Northern France, the bucket urns can most easily be identified as developments from the pottery of the preceding period in Britain. The element of continuity which they may, therefore, represent is also to be noted in other aspects of these burials. The universal adoption of cremation seems to be the culmination of a trend which had begun several centuries earlier, and flat cemeteries of cremations first appear in Britain well before 2000 BC. Furthermore, not all of the new 'urnfields' are flat cemeteries but some are laid into existing round barrows, as happens at Latch Farm (Dorset), and others are associated with newly-built barrows, as is the case at Itford Hill (Sussex). Sites such as these suggest an important element of continuity from the preceding era. This conclusion is underlined by the continued occupation of the settlements at Shearplace Hill, Rams Hill and Trevisker, and it is probable that many stone-built settlements of this period known in the South-West peninsular were first occupied a century or two earlier as well. Some of the settlements were by now large enough to be described as

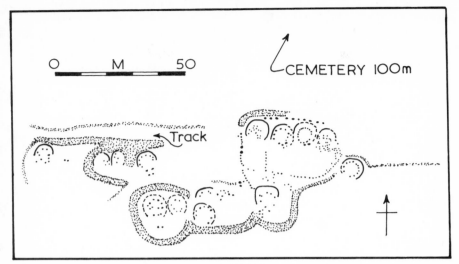

The settlement at Itford Hill, Sussex, c.1,100 BC.

hamlets or villages. At Itford Hill a series of embanked enclosures each contained two or more huts, the whole settlement comprising at least thirteen buildings. Many of these were not used as houses but as workshops or stores, but at least four families are thought to have made up the community here. A less compact group of enclosures at Plumpton Plain (Sussex) similarly contains two or three huts each and represents a community of three or four families. In both these instances we have, apparently, individual family enclosures which are grouped together to form a settlement or community of larger size.

Elsewhere in Southern England, there were communities of similar size, which were brought together within a single enclosure. At Thorny Down a rectangular enclosure was occupied by nine or ten huts, while excavations at Rams Hill suggest that there may have been a larger settlement there, although in its latest phase of occupation it was unenclosed. So far, excavations in a quarter of the enclosure have revealed two circular huts, possibly separated by a boundary fence, and six small square structures of a type normally identified as the remains of granaries. In contrast to these settlements there are also a number of isolated farmsteads, in which two or three huts represent the home and workplace of a single farmer and his family. Chalton

(Hants), carbon dated to about 1300 BC, and Eldons Seat (Dorset) dated to perhaps c.700 BC, are good examples of the type and suggest that it persisted with little or no change in form throughout the period.

On all these sites the huts are timber-built, and apart from the small four-post structures at Rams Hill, they are circular in plan. In some cases their roof rafters were supported by a circle of timber uprights set in some distance from the outer wall, while in others the roof and wall supports seem to be a single set of uprights which fulfill both functions. In size they vary from about 15 to 35 feet in diameter, the larger often revealing traces of occupation, the smaller sometimes producing evidence that they were not used as houses. One interesting feature of several huts at Itford Hill and one at Rams Hill is the appearance of a projecting porch supported on two pairs of uprights, which must have provided much better protection from cold draughts and rain than the unprotected doorways of earlier huts. Huts of circular plan, with timber roof supports and sometimes porches, are found in the South-West peninsula at this time, but here the walls are built of stone. For this reason they have very often survived to the present day, and at first sight create the impression that they, and the settlements in which they are found, are totally different from the timber houses of Southern England. In fact here too we have a pattern of settlement which

A stone-built hut of c.1,200 BC on Dartmoor.

includes enclosed villages, settlements comprising a series of family enclosures, and isolated, individual farmsteads.

On Dartmoor fine examples of all three types are to be found. At Riders Rings and Grimspound there are large enclosures protected in each case by a very substantial stone wall. Inside are circular stone huts, between twenty and thirty of them, some standing close to the wall for protection from the elements, others sited in the open space at the centre of the enclosure. Even larger numbers of huts are found in some of the unenclosed settlements, like that at Standon Down, where nearly seventy stone huts have been noted. Many of these are linked together by stretches of straight stone walling, so that a complex of enclosures and related huts has been formed. These are very different indeed to the tiny farmsteads like Rippon Tor with a single circular hut, or Blissmoor with three such buildings, but all of these South-Western settlements seem to be local adaptations, in stone, of settlement and house types found elsewhere in Southern Britain. Further north and north-west different types of settlements were probably

The enclosed village of Grimspound, Dartmoor.

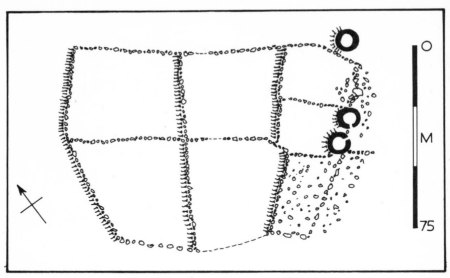

A farmstead and its fields, c.1,200 BC, at Blissmoor, Dartmoor.

being occupied. We know little of them at present but apart from occupied caves in Wales, Northern England and Scotland, there were also hilltop settlements to which we shall refer shortly.

On Dartmoor it seems likely that the different types of settlement reflect differences in the farming economy, and the three settlement types are found in three reasonably distinct areas, on the south, west and east of the moor. The enclosed villages of the south have only small cultivation plots built against the inside face of the surrounding wall, and were clearly dependent for the greater part of their food supply on cattle and sheep. The same must be broadly true of the unenclosed settlements found mainly on the wetter, western, fringes of the moor, and the complex of irregular enclosures associated with the groups of huts in them were probably pens for animals rather than cultivation areas. Only around the isolated farmsteads on the eastern fringes are there clear traces of contemporary fields in which crops were grown. Here, small squarish fields totalling between one and three acres in area, surround the huts of the farmer and indicate that the fertile brown soil of the area was exploited in a mixed economy based on corn and cattle.

Similar fields of the same date were found further west at Gwithian in Cornwall, and field systems around the settlements at Plumpton

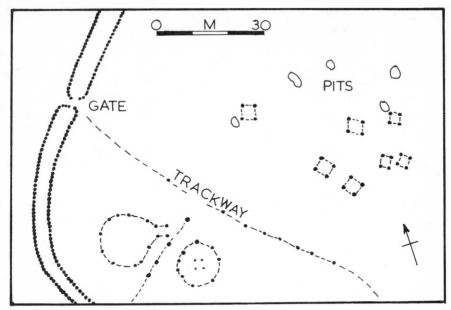

A corner of the settlement at Rams Hill, Berks, c.1,100-900 BC.

Plain and Itford Hill are probably contemporary with them. At Gwithian plough marks survive in the sub-soil, showing that the fields had been cross-ploughed, and that around the edges of the field where the plough could not till the soil, wooden spades had been used to turn it over. Much of the crops grown in these fields were winter-sown hulled barley, but emmer wheat accounted for perhaps a fifth of the crop and as conditions deteriorated to a wetter climate from 1000 BC onwards, its importance grew. From about 1300 BC onwards short bronze sickles were available for reaping, their length suggesting that only the ears were cut and harvested. The crop was then stored in pits which, in some instances, as at Minnis Bay (Kent), for example, were lined with matted rushwork and covered by a wooden lid. At Itford Hill nearly twelve pounds of barley were found still stored in one such pit, the total capacity of which was about seventy pounds of corn. Whether or not the onset of wetter conditions encouraged the adoption of granary buildings raised above the ground on four or six heavy timber uprights is uncertain, but buildings of this sort seem to appear from perhaps 1100 BC onwards at Rams Hill, from between 1000 and 700 BC (carbon dates) at Grimthorpe (Yorkshire), and shortly after 700 BC at Ivinghoe (Bucks).

Certainly the changing climate can be directly related to both the prevailing pastoral economy at the beginning of the period and the change of emphasis which took place in it in the centuries after 1000 BC. The importance of cattle rearing in the centuries before 1300 BC shows no signs of decline in the centuries following that date. At Fengate a very extensive area of ditched enclosures and droveways of this period has recently been excavated, and is probably to be associated with the careful winter management of herds, which in summer were grazed on the grass of the Fen islands. Even more extensive systems of ditches and enclosures are found scattered across Wessex and the South Downs, with large areas defined by 'ranch boundaries' as pastureland. These boundaries and associated cross-dykes are directly related to a series of roughly rectangular enclosures up to two and a half acres in size, surrounded by a ditch and bank and with one or two entrances. These reveal no signs of permanent habitation, and in the case of the example at Portsdown there is good evidence to suggest that cattle were brought to the enclosure to be slaughtered and the best of the meat taken away—presumably to some nearby settlement. Evidence for the same practice might be identified at Harrow Hill too, although in this case the enclosure may date as late as 600 - 500 BC.

The importance of cattle, and the way in which they were used, is further attested by the evidence from settlement sites, where bone awls and needles and flint scrapers survive in sufficient numbers to indicate large-scale preparation and working of hides. At Itford Hill and Rams Hill cattle dominated the bone samples, and at the latter careful analysis has shown that the animals were probably used for hides and dairy products as well as for meat. The same picture emerges from the animal bones found at Eldon's Seat (Dorset), belonging to the period just after 700 BC. Here, however, the balance between sheep and cattle was much closer than on earlier sites, with cattle accounting for 51% of the animal population and sheep 41%. The increasing importance of sheep as the climate became wetter is documented also by other remains found in the settlements of the early first millennium. Minnis Bay and Plumpton Plain (Site B) produced loomweights and spindle whorls testifying to both the spinning and weaving of wool, and at Eldon's Seat bone wool-carding combs amplify the evidence of the ani-

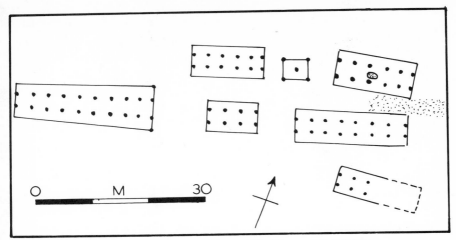

Long timber houses inside the fort at Crickley Hill, Glos, c.700-600 BC.

mal bones. Overall, the evidence points to a gradual increase in the importance of sheep at the expense of cattle. The pastoral enclosures mentioned earlier, however, remained in use down to the close of the period and it is a matter of great interest and importance that several of them subsequently became the site of hill-forts. Well known examples of this sequence are to be found at Hollingbury and Highdown (Sussex), and it has been suggested that these relatively small and early hill-forts were, like their predecessors on the same sites, an integral part of the pastoral economy. The principal difference between the earlier and later enclosures is that the later ones have more imposing earthworks which allow us to describe them as 'defences', and this presumably implies increasing hostility between neighbouring communities in the period around 700 BC. Whether or not such a state of affairs was the result on the one hand of a growth of population, and on the other of the changing climate which may have led to greater pressure on the less marginal farming land, is uncertain.

It is clear, however, that outside Southern England, the growth of warfare began well before the end of the second millennium BC, and that it resulted in the development of heavily defended hill-top settlements, or hill-forts. The rampart of Norton Fitzwarren in Somerset was built sometime before 1200 BC—the date of manufacture of a hoard of bronze bangles which were buried in it. At Mam Tor in Derbyshire, huts inside the defences have been carbon dated to about

A looped spearhead with a modern shaft inserted.

1300-1100 BC and have produced pottery and metalwork of this and the following period. Grimthorpe hill-fort (Yorkshire) is carbon dated to about 1000-700 BC, Dinorben (Denbigh) to the same period, and several Scottish hill-forts have produced isolated carbon dates of this order. Elsewhere, evidence of considerable occupation in the period c.1000-700 BC has been found inside hill-fort defences. At the Breiddin (Montgomery) site various bronzes tools and weapons of this period have been recovered, and the same is true of South Cadbury (Somerset) and several other hill-forts. Extensive traces of settlement have been discovered at Trapain Law (East Lothian) and Crickley Hill (Glos), including at the latter a series of rectangular buildings up to 80 feet long. The accumulating evidence points quite clearly to the development of substantial hilltop settlements in Northern and Western Britain in the period between 1300 and 700 BC, and although the man-made defences of these settlements have still to be dated in most cases, there can be no real doubt that the sites were chosen primarily for their defensive advantages. The evidence which these sites supply for the increase in warfare is supplemented by that of the metalwork of this

The skeleton of one of two young men brought down by spears c.1,100 BC, near Tormarton, Glos.

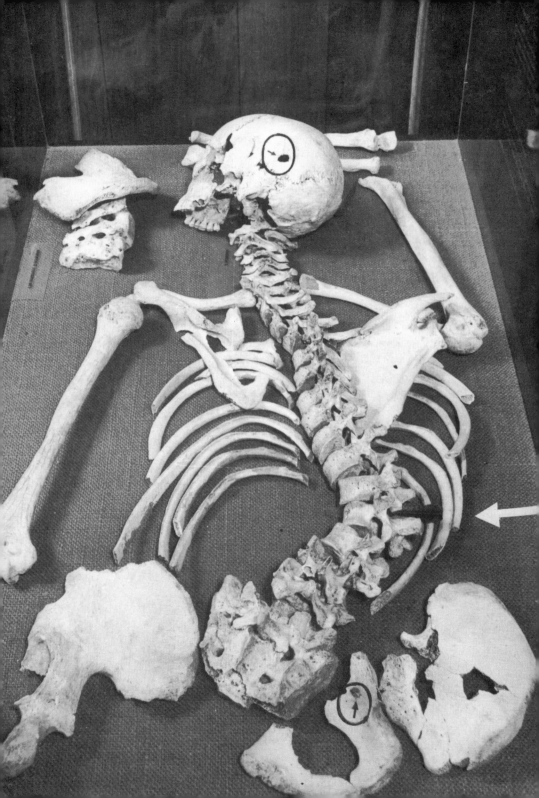

period, which takes on an increasingly military flavour. At the beginning of the period the short daggers of the preceding era were joined by longer 'swords' with narrower blades, and by an increasing number of looped spearheads. Two young men who fell victims to such spearheads were recently discovered at Tormarton (Glos). In the last century of the second millennium, imports of heavy bronze swords from the Continent, and possibly the arrival of some of the warriors who used them, led to the development of British leaf-shaped swords. We know of no bronze armour in Britain which might have protected the user of such weapons, but circular shields of leather have survived, as have ceremonial ones of bronze and heavy wooden ones which may have been the formers on which the leather was shaped rather than the practical shields themselves. A warrior holding one of these shields is to be seen in a wooden model of a group of four standing on a boat, found at Roos Carr (Yorkshire).

It has been suggested that in the period after 800 BC, it is perhaps possible to recognise regional variations in the use of weapons of war in England. Over much of Central England the spear seems to have been the principal weapon, while further north and east swords were more popular; in South-East England both types of weapon seem to have been used. Whether or not these differences really existed is difficult to establish, but if they did then they might imply quite different methods of warfare, for the spear is essentially a medium-range weapon, and the sword a short-range one. Certainly there were regional variations in metalworking, with distinctive varieties of tools and weapons being produced in several parts of England, Wales and Ireland. The ubiquitous socketed axe, in widespread use from about 1000 BC onwards, was particularly susceptible to local and regional variation.

A looped and socketed axe from Lee Common, Bucks.

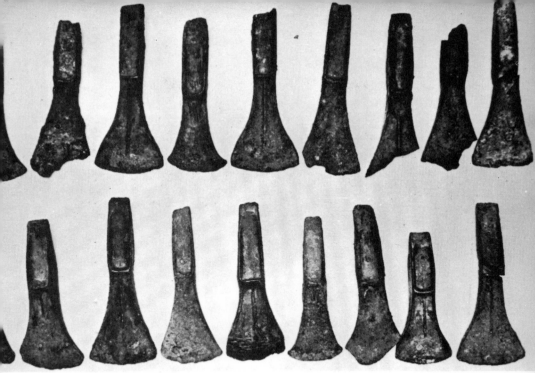

A hoard of palstaves from Burnham, Bucks c.1,300-1,200 BC.

The Irish bronzeworkers, on the other hand, produced many items which were exclusive to them; bronze buckets and cauldrons, rattle pendants, and trumpets—and the same invention and craftsmanship is seen in Irish goldwork which ranged from thin sheet-gold boxes and finely made pins to large neck-rings and collars. In England there was little goldworking after the decline of the South-Western ornament-hoards of gold and bronze bangles, pins and rings made between about 1300 and 1100 BC.

These hoards of metalwork were by no means a new feature in British prehistory, but in the centuries after 1000 BC there is a marked increase in the frequency of hoards, which is thought to reflect the growing insecurity of the times. Some of these hoards, particularly those in Ireland, seem to be votive depositions made for religious reasons, but others are the belongings of itinerant bronzesmiths and were presumably hidden at a time when danger threatened. These 'founders' hoards' contain not only stocks of axes and other bronze goods to trade but also broken tools and weapons to be used for scrap, the hammers, tongs and sets used by the smith himself, some of his

109

moulds, and ingots of metal ready to be melted down in a crucible. An excellent example of the group is the hoard from the cave at Heathery Burn (Durham). Stray hoards like these, found in the countryside, presumably point to the continued employment of itinerant smiths, but by the end of the period there are perhaps some signs that resident smiths could be found in some settlements. Several of the hill-fort sites which have produced artifacts of the early first millennium BC have also produced contemporary hoards of metalwork, and a founder's hoard was buried on the occupation site at Minnis Bay (Kent). At Jarlshof (Shetland) clear evidence of a bronzesmith at work in the settlement has been recovered. How these men obtained their raw materials is not known, though by this time there must have been a constant supply of scrap from broken and damaged artifacts, but, as the use of iron was gradually introduced, the acquisition of raw metal became somewhat easier, simply because sources of iron are more widespread in Britain than sources of copper and tin.

Just when the first iron was used in Britain, and whether it was brought in as ready-made goods from the continent or smelted and worked here, is still unknown. Seventh century hoards of metalwork from Sompting (Sussex) and Llyn Fawr (Glamorgan), however, have produced ironwork, and further seventh century finds of iron artifacts have been made at Sheepen Hill (Essex) and Staple Howe (Yorkshire). There can be little doubt that the secret of working iron was brought into Britain by the people to whose culture we have given the name Hallstatt. Contacts were maintained between Britain and the Continent throughout the period from 1300 to 700 BC, and in the earlier part of the period are represented by imported *palstaves* from Brittany and Iberia, and the 'ornament hoards' inspired by German examples. Later we have the introduction of Hallstatt swords and razors and finally the arrival of iron-working together with a wide range of horse-trappings and cart-fittings found in the Llyn Fawr and Heathery Burn hoards as well as several others. The appearance of horse-fittings and new sword types is particularly important and marks the arrival on our shores of new invaders—Hallstatt warriors—in the second half of the seventh century BC. New methods of warfare and a new material (iron) for the manufacture of weapons, together with the established trends towards defended settlements and more frequent recourse to warfare, mark the end of one age and the beginning of another.

650–150 BC

The new era which began in the middle of the seventh century BC saw the differences between the highland and lowland zones of Britain increasingly emphasised. The influence of the natural environment was not the only factor at work in this situation, and the accessibility of the south and east to both ideas and immigrants from the Continent does much to explain the innovations appearing in the lowland zone throughout the period, which contrasts strongly with the overall conservatism of the societies of the highland zone.

At the beginning of the period, the continental contacts of the south and east are represented not only by immigrant 'Halstatt' warriors but by imported swords, horse trappings, razors and pieces of jewellery. Some of the latter are brooches of Italian manufacture, and also, a handful of Italian and Greek painted vases of this period have been found in England. In the fifth and fourth centuries imported daggers are more common than swords, and bracelets and brooches were obtained from the nearer parts of Western Europe. But the ancient Atlantic trade-route also came into prominence at this time as Carthaginian and Greek explorers journeyed to Britain and were followed by merchants trading for tin. Rare finds of Iberian bronzework are more plentiful, but stray finds of Greek coins corroborate the brief accounts of Herodotus, Pytheas, Diodorus and Strabo, and one of the valuable ingots of tin for which the Greek sailors travelled so far from home was found many years ago at the mouth of the river Fal, at St. Mawes, Cornwall. It was of course from Cornwall that the Greeks, and indeed the British, obtained their supplies of tin, but iron was much more widely distributed and seems to have been extracted and worked by local smiths throughout Britain. Evidence of iron smelting and working, such as slag and iron ore, are not uncommon finds on domestic sites of the period, and at Kestor (Devon) and West Brandon (Durham) bowl hearths in which the smelting was carried out have been found. Whether or not some of the larger settlements employed spe-

111

An Italian brooch of the 900-800 BC, found at Berkhamsted, Herts.

cialist smiths is uncertain, although at Kestor, a settlement of about twenty huts, the evidence of iron working was indeed concentrated in a single building. Equally, the superb swords and daggers, and their fine bronze scabbards, of the fourth and third centuries BC point to the existence of specialist craftsmen in both iron and bronze. Other crafts which come into prominence in this period include weaving, shale working, salt production and probably carpentry. Apart from the evidence of animal bones, increasing numbers of loomweights, spindle whorls and bone wool-combs attest to the growing importance of wool and weaving. At Staple Howe (Yorks), where loomweights and spindle whorls were found inside the settlement, at least one circular hut seems to have been set aside as a weaving shed in which an upright loom was erected. Contemporary drawings on pottery used by Hallstatt people in Hungary show women using this type of loom, as well as spinning with a whorl. The construction of looms required the services of a carpenter, and the increased range and strength of tools made available by the use of iron must have stimulated this craft, but first-hand evidence, of course, rarely survives. In contrast, we have both the finished products and evidence of the way in which they were

112

A tin ingot found in the mouth of the river Fal at St. Mawes.

manufactured, in the case of the shale industry, centred on the Isle of Purbeck, Dorset. Rings and bracelets were the principal products, carved from discs of the raw material with simple flint blades. At Eldon's Seat, where over seven-hundred pieces of shale in various stages of working were found, it was clear that the craft formed a secondary element in the economy of the farmstead. Other sites in the Isle of Purbeck have yielded evidence of salt extraction from seawater by a lengthy process involving the use of both evaporation and boiling pans. The salt industry seems to have been spread around the southern and eastern shores of England and further sites are known in Hampshire and Lincolnshire, as well as very extensive extraction sites of a later date along the coast of Essex. Evidence from the continent suggests that the salt was probably moulded and traded in cakes of a standard size and value, and as a preservative for meat it would certainly have been a much-sought-after commodity.

Beef seems to have remained the principal meat consumed in Britain, although the number of sheep kept seems to have grown and the number of cattle to have declined, from the earlier periods. At Eldons Seat, where two groups of animal bones of the seventh and fifth centuries respectively could be compared, the number of sheep (as a percentage of the total animal population of the farm) rose from 40% to 60%,

A bone wool-comb of about the 6th century BC.

while the cattle dropped from 50% to less than 30%. Not all farms reveal the same balance between sheep and cattle of course, and on some, cattle continue to be the most numerous animal, but the general trend from cattle to sheep is uniform throughout the country. Sheep, however, seem to have been produced as much for wool as for meat, and cattle of course also produce approximately seven times as much meat per carcass as do sheep. The increasing production of sheep, however, was not undertaken primarily to increase the amount of meat available. Apart from wool production, it has been suggested that the popularity of sheep in the first millennium BC is directly related to developments in agriculture and cereal production.

Sheep were easier to maintain, particularly on the chalk downlands, than were cattle, and they were needed in large numbers to manure the thousands of acres of arable land which spread across the downland in this period. In some areas the squarish fields of this period, originally bounded by stones, fences, hedges or gullies, still survive and are linked by trackways to the settlements from which they were once farmed. Cross-ploughing was employed, as in earlier periods, but the ploughs now had iron ploughshares and it is thought that a pair of oxen could have ploughed an average-sized field in a day. A more important innovation, however, was the introduction of hulled barley and the re-introduction of wheat as a major crop. The particular type of wheat which was now grown was spelt, which, like hulled barley, could be sown in the autumn and therefore harvested somewhat earlier than either naked barley or emmer wheat. At the same time small quantities of other cereals—rye, oats and clubwheat—were being introduced so that the whole process of cereal production was gradually being refined and improved.

'Celtic' fields on Pertwood Down.

In Southern England the storage pits and four- or six-post granaries, in which the grain was stored for the winter, are some of the most
characteristic features of the settlements of this period. Individual
farmsteads commonly comprise an enclosure of between two and ten
acres surrounded by a palisade or ditch and bank, inside which are one
or two circular huts. The main dwelling house is a timber hut of about
40 feet diameter with a double row of wall and roof supports and a
four-post porch protecting the doorway. Beyond the hut are dozens of
storage pits, several small granary buildings, drying racks, and the
working hollows where the corn was parched before threshing. Farmsteads of this sort, like those at Little Woodbury and Gussage All
Saints, emphasise very clearly the important part which cereals played
in the economy of Southern England at this time. Similar agricultural
installations are to be found in some of the villages occasionally discovered in lowland Britain, like those at Little Waltham (Essex) and
Heathrow (Middlesex). The latter, now buried under a concrete run-
way of the airport, was a village of almost five acres containing some
ten to fifteen circular huts with its own shrine, surrounded by a

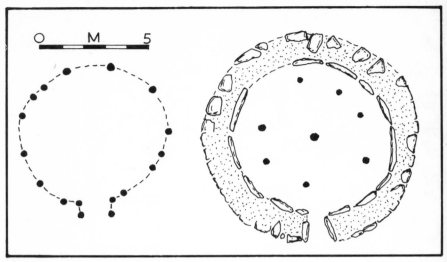

Timber and stone houses at Eldon's Seat and Kestor.

ditched and banked enclosure. Villages of four and five times this size are known in Wessex but little is known of the details of their buildings and other features since none has been extensively excavated. Further west still, in the South-West peninsula, a variety of settlement-types are to be found, most of which seem to fall into the category of hamlets or small villages. Some, like Bodrifty (Cornwall) are not unlike earlier settlements on Dartmoor, with ten or a dozen huts linked together by stretches of walling.

Others, like Kestor (Devon), have huts scattered throughout an integrated field system. Generally later in date and perhaps reflecting changes in both the structure of society and methods of warfare, are a variety of small earthwork-defended settlements. At Castle Dore, for example, a one and a half acre enclosure contained about fifteen huts, and this is probably typical of many similar sites in the region. Along the coasts, rocky headlands like Gurnards Head were cut-off by defensive earthworks and the exposed slopes thus protected were occupied by similar numbers of huts. Here, as one might expect, the huts were often at least partially built of stone, and lacked the porch so characteristic of their contemporaries to the east. Similarly, storage pits and granaries are not common features of these villages, and surviving field systems are small compared with those of Wessex. The annexes

116

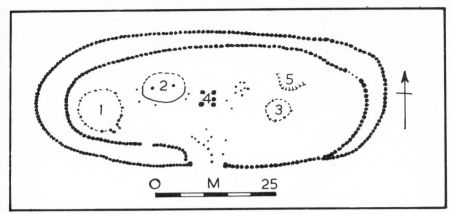

The farmstead at Staple Howe, Yorks.

outside the settlements and hill-slope enclosures of a clearly non-defensive type both emphasise the greater importance of animals, particularly cattle, in the farm economy of the South-West.

Little is known of either farmsteads or villages in Wales at this time, although the enclosed village of stone huts at Castell Odo (Caerns), replacing an earlier open settlement, has no close parallels in the South-West peninsula and suggests that here too a distinctive regional variation of settlement type might have developed. The same conclusion emerges from excavations at Beckford in the Severn Valley north of Gloucester, where a remarkable settlement of about ten acres comprises a series of individual ditched compounds, each with its own circular hut and pits for grain storage, rubbish and sewage. The houses here are of the usual circular plan, their walls built of small stakes set in a shallow groove, except at the entrance where large timber posts were inserted to carry the door. Each house possessed one or more clay-lined water 'tanks'. The evidence recovered so far suggests that cereals were more important here than further west, and that sheep and cattle were the main domesticates.

In Northern Britain we have more abundant evidence of both farmsteads and villages, the earliest of which, like Staple Howe, Huckhoe and Burnswark, are enclosed by palisades. Some of these, like Huckhoe and West Brandon, later had their palisades replaced by earthwork defences, a sequence of development noticed in Southern Britain too, at Little Woodbury. The farmsteads in the North may comprise

117

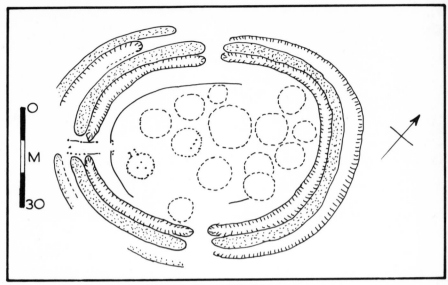

The enclosed village at Braidwood Fort, Midlothian.

between one and four circular huts, often built with two or even three concentric rings of wall and roof supports but only occasionally with a projecting porch. Apart from the rare discovery of four- and five-post granaries at Huckhoe and Staple Howe, and a few quernstones from other sites, there is little evidence of agriculture. On the other hand many of the farmsteads have enclosures which were far larger than any domestic needs might dictate, and some such as Burradon have an outer enclosure too, and it seems likely that the enclosures served as cattle pounds as well as settlement areas. Small villages of ten to fifteen huts, at Hayhope (Roxburgh) and Braidwood (Midlothian) for example, are much more densely built-over inside enclosures, which are often little or no bigger than those of individual farmsteads elsewhere. Here again, however, there is no evidence that the larger communities which these settlements represent depended to any notable degree on cereal production. Further north and west early examples of farmsteads with stone-built circular huts, discovered at Kilphedir (Sutherland), Jarlshof and Clickhimin (Shetland) give way to more heavily defended types of settlement in many cases. At Clickhimin the roundhouse farmstead is replaced by a ring-fort or *dun* in which a stone-built wall defends a settlement occupying timber-ranges built onto its

118

The single rampart and ditch (with counterscarp) of Liddington Castle, Wilts.

inside face. Although little is still known about their history, many *duns* of various sorts are known in western and northern Scotland and there is no doubt that they originate in the middle centuries of the first millennium BC. The same appears to be true of the so-called *crannogs*, artificial islands of brushwood pegged into the marshy ground around the edge of lakes by vertical posts, and occupied by a single circular hut. Like the *duns*, the *crannogs* seem to represent farmsteads whose inhabitants found it necessary to take extra precautions against attack; from Roman authors of a few centuries later we learn that these Western areas of Scotland were open to attack by pirates from Ireland and the Western Isles, some of whom still practised cannibalism!

Although cannibalism may have been restricted to the western fringes of Britain (and some believe it was more widespread) hostilities were certainly not. To what extent the palisades and earthworks which enclosed farmsteads and villages were defensive is difficult to assess, but there can be no doubting the primarily defensive role of the great ramparts and ditches which surround the hill-forts of this period. We have already seen the beginning of defended hill-top villages in the preceding era, but from the sixth century onwards they grow in size, complexity, and most of all in numbers. The Ordnance Survey lists over three thousand hill-forts in Britain, but many of these are defended farmsteads or hamlets like those we mentioned earlier in the South-West peninsula. If we consider only the largest of these forts, however,

119

covering more than fifteen acres, we still find about a hundred and fifty of them concentrated in Southern England and up the Severn Valley, as well as many others of between eight and fifteen acres which probably represent very similar types of settlement. Further forts are of course to be found further north, particularly in Scotland. Some of the earliest Scottish forts such as Finavon (Angus) have 'vitrified' ramparts, in which stone defences laced with timbers have been deliberately fired so that the lumps of stone have become vitrified into great masses of rock, much more difficult to undermine or breach than an unvitrified rampart. Timber-laced stone ramparts are found further south in Yorkshire and Wales, and in England the earliest forts such as Grimthorpe and Ivinghoe, have so-called box ramparts built of timber and infilled with earth. By the sixth century an earthern rampart was being added to the rear of this type of defence, and by the following century the timber 'box' had given way to a single timber revetment backed by a substantial rampart. These changes no doubt took place in the light of experience and two problems which must have recurred with all these types of defence were the necessity of replacing timbers every forty or fifty years (at most), and the gradual erosion of the lip of the ditch which normally fronted the rampart, so that the rampart eventually began to topple into the ditch.

The dump (or Glacis) rampart which was introduced in the third century perhaps overcame both problems at once, by dispensing with timberwork altogether and building an earth rampart which formed a continuous gradient with the slope of the ditch. This type of defence

The multiple ramparts of Battlesbury Hill-Fort (Wilts).

also had the advantage of greatly increasing the elevation of defenders over attackers, who by the time they reached the bottom of the ditch were often as much as 50 or 60 feet below the defenders on the top of the rampart above. At the same time entrances were elaborated and attackers going for the east gate of Torberry (Sussex), for example, found themselves in a narrow inturned passage nearly sixty feet long, and no doubt overlooked by defenders lining the walls on either side. Further earthworks beyond the gateway often made a direct frontal attack on it almost impossible, whilst height advantage of the defenders was turned to good use by extending the horizontal depth of the defences and adding an outer rampart and ditch.

For a long time it was thought that hill-forts were essentially places of refuge for man and beast in times of war, but there is now ample evidence that many hill-forts were occupied for long periods of time by large populations. Some of the Northern and Western forts where remains of stone built huts still survive on the surface, give an idea of how large these populations could be. Eildon Hill (Roxburgh) had perhaps five hundred huts, Yevering (Northumberland) about a hundred and fifty, and Tre'r Ceiri (Caerns) up to eighty. Not all these huts need have been houses, nor occupied all at the same time, but it is difficult to escape the conclusion that we must think in terms of communities of several hundred people. In terms of size alone, these forts might therefore qualify as townships—many of the smaller towns of Roman Britain centuries later, would have had populations of only a few hundred. Excavations at forts in Southern England and the Welsh border-

The Hill-Fort at Tre'r Ceiri (Caerns).

lands are beginning to reveal, furthermore, the extent to which these were well-ordered communities, subject to a certain degree of planning and control. We have already seen the orderly arrangement of oblong buildings which lined a roadway inside the fort on Crickley Hill (Glos), and further examples of rectangular buildings erected in neat rows have been discovered at Credenhill and Croft Ambrey in Herefordshire. Here, the buildings are the square four-post variety usually identified as granaries but almost certainly representing houses on some sites. Pairs and groups of similar four-post buildings, aligned either on each other or on the rampart have been discovered inside the hill-fort at Grimthorpe (Yorkshire). These planned interiors are not confined to the north and west however. At Danebury (Hants) four rows of six-post huts have been excavated, aligned along streets and backed by clusters of pits. Streets have also been noted inside the hill-forts of Maiden Castle and Hod Hill, and at Chalbury (Dorset), many of the huts can be seen to form an evenly spaced row of buildings which follows the line of the rampart, probably around its entire circuit.

These signs of communal planning, together with the organisation of labour needed to build and maintain the hill-fort defences, point clearly to the emergence of some sort of authority who could control and direct the activities of a community of several hundred people. At the same time the complex and progressive development of hill-fort defences between 600 BC and 200 BC was clearly the product of a period of considerable unrest which affected most parts of Britain. No doubt these changes in social organisation on the one hand and social behaviour on the other were closely related, but they may both have been the products of other factors. The onset of a colder and wetter climate and the extension of blanket peat over upland areas formerly occupied must have increased the pressure on the better areas of arable and pastureland. At the same time the refinements to cereal production in southern Britain may have engendered the growth of population which seems to be represented by the great number of settlements of this period. Taken together with the arrival of immigrant farmers and warriors from the continent, these various factors may together have operated to bring about increasing land pressure and the emergence of warfare and war leaders that such a situation often brings in its wake. By the end of the third century BC it is possi-

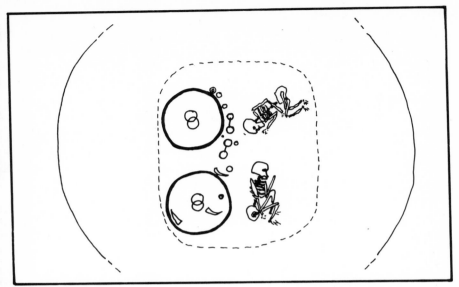

The cart burial at Danes Graves, Yorks.

ble to identify a number of important hill-forts in central Wessex which seem to control territories of up to fifty square miles. Other hill-forts in these territories are in decline or abandoned. Tribal chief-doms, which may well have existed before this time, can now be not only firmly recognised but also identified with a specific tract of terri-tory. The same phenomenon can be observed along the South Downs and in the Chilterns, and may well remain to be recognised in other parts of Southern Britain. The existence and power of the chieftains is demonstrated by their forts and the territory we believe can be attrib-uted to them, but it is also represented by some of the superb weapons and shields of the third century onwards, by the appearance of warrior emblems, such as the boar, and by some of the richer burials which are found in parts of Britain. The most notable of those are the cart burials of eastern Yorkshire, which have parallels and almost certainly direct antecedents in Burgundy. Extensive cemeteries of low barrows cover-ing inhumations include rare examples in which a complete cart has been buried. In the so-called 'King's Barrow' at Arras in Northern France there were not only the remains of the dismantled cart (wheels, lynch pins, terret-rings) and various horse trappings but the skeletons of two horses as well. Two pigs heads were also found in this grave,

123

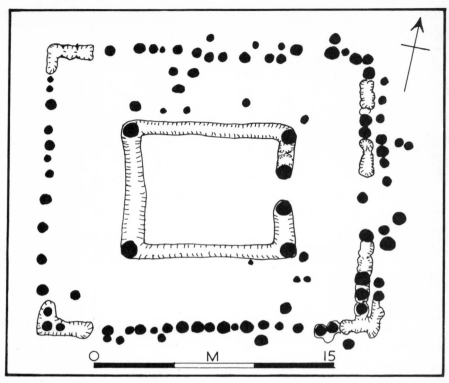

The timber temple at Heathrow, Middlesex.

and another in a cart burial at Garton Slack, as well as the complete
skeleton of a pig in a warrior burial at North Grimston (Yorkshire);
these finds support the connection between the pig or boar and the warrior class.

Apart from these burials, and a handful of isolated warrior burials
from other areas and belonging to the very end of the period, burials of
any kind are not common in this period and those that do occur have
very few grave-goods. Some of the earlier burials continue the rites of
the preceding era, with cremations with or without coarse urns under
low barrows. A small cemetery of this type at Ampleforth Moor (Yorkshire) is carbon dated to between 600 BC and 500 BC. Later burials are
mainly inhumations, and occur in small cists and sometimes re-used
storage pits on settlement sites. But the scarcity of burials, at a time
when the evidence points to a marked increase in population, is not-

124

able and significant. Stray human bones occur on many settlement sites and it is possible that bodies were exposed either in or near to the settlement. On the whole this seems more likely than the widespread practice of cannibalism.

Ritual cannibalism may have played a role in Britain at this time, however, and certainly if we are to believe Roman authors, human sacrifice was not uncommon. The Druids, of whom we read so much and know so little, were certainly active in this period and the large quantity of metalwork, bronze and gold, found in rivers and bogs almost certainly includes much that was deposited originally for religious reasons rather than hidden for safety or in panic. In recent years there has been accumulating evidence of places of ritual during this era, the most interesting of which perhaps are at Navan and Dun Ailinne in Ireland. At both these sites earthwork enclosures have proved to contain circular timber settings which were eventually covered by cairns. Their resemblance to much earlier ritual sites in both Ireland and England is uncanny and may imply that in Ireland at least the 'henge' tradition never entirely died out in the second millennium BC. In Wales the settlement inside the hill-fort at Moel-y-Gaer seems to have had its own shrine in the form of a stone-filled oval pit surrounded by a circle of seven posts, whilst in the roughly contemporary settlement at Heathrow there was a built shrine with a verandah and cellar. Several other hill-forts have produced the remains of buildings plausibly identified as shrines, but the surviving remains in each case appear to belong to the following period. Most sacred places of this era must forever elude us for, apart from rivers and bogs, we know from the Roman authors that many sanctuaries were sacred groves, no recognisable evidence of which is likely to be discovered. The fact that we know much at all about religious beliefs and rites at this time is due largely to the combined evidence of later (8th-10th century AD) Irish sources and only slightly later (1st-4th century AD) Roman ones. In other words, by the middle of the second century BC we stand on the verge of written history for the first time in Britain. Fleeting references in Greek and Roman authors are soon to be amplified by the first-hand accounts of Caesar, and by the first 'written' records of the British themselves in the form of inscribed coinage. But for these records we should be hard pressed to chronicle the dramatic events which were to take place in Britain in the last two centuries before the Roman conquest.

CHAPTER EIGHT

150 BC – AD 43

In Julius Caesar's *Gallic Wars* we are told that the people inhabiting the coastal areas of South-East England in the mid first century BC were invaders from Northern France and Belgium, part of the tribe known as the Belgae. They came initially to plunder but eventually settled in Britain and became farmers. Archaeologically we can recognise these first adventurers by the Gallic coins which they brought with them from about 150 BC and which are today found scattered in Kent, Essex, the Thames Valley, the Chilterns and along the coast of Sussex. By shortly after 100 BC coins of broadly the same types, and certainly derived from Gallic examples, were being struck in Britain and seem to indicate that Belgae were controlling, or at least operating in, the area of England east of a line drawn between Southampton Water and the Wash. Their numbers were swollen about 60 BC by a major influx of refugees from Gaul, undoubtedly fleeing from Caesar himself. Thereafter, coins struck in Britain become increasingly distinctive of certain areas and certain tribes, and it is from the brief inscriptions which they carry and the changing distributions of the various tribal coinages that we can trace the struggle for power which engulfed the whole of Southern England from about 50 BC until the Roman invasion of 43 AD.

The success of the Belgic tribes in this struggle seems to have been due more to their ability to organise themselves politically and militarily than to any new weapons of war which they introduced. Archaeologically, the organised might of the Belgic tribes is represented by a series of settlements of a type entirely new to Britain—the so-called *oppida*. These were vast areas of land enclosed by a series of huge ditches or dykes. One of the earliest known to us, at Wheathampstead in Hertfordshire, was about a hundred acres in size at the time that it was attacked by Caesar in 54 BC. Its defensive ditch was a hundred and thirty feet wide and forty deep. In contrast the *oppidum* at Camulodunum (modern Colchester) had grown to over twelve and a half

Coins of the Catuvellauni and Dobunni.

square miles by 43 AD, yet its defensive dykes were no more than forty feet wide and fifteen deep. These two *oppida* were, at these two different periods, the capital of a single tribe—the Catuvellauni—and the vastly increased area and less massive defences of Camulodunum reflect the growth of the wealth and power of this tribe in the space of a century. By no means the whole of the area enclosed by the dykes of an *oppida* was occupied by buildings. At both Verulamium (St. Albans) and Camulodunum some areas were set aside as cemeteries, and it is clear that others were grazing land and cultivation plots. Further areas were occupied by the mints producing tribal coinage and by other metal working activities. Scattered amongst these were clusters of huts, some circular in plan, others rectangular, but all having only clay or chalk floors and clay or wattle walls. Yet the undistinguished building remains should not mislead us; there is little doubt that it was in one and two-roomed huts of this simple type that the Belgic aristocracy lived, for from the rubbish pits around some of them have come large quantities of imported glass and pottery from Italy and Gaul and fragments of amphorae which would originally have arrived here full

127

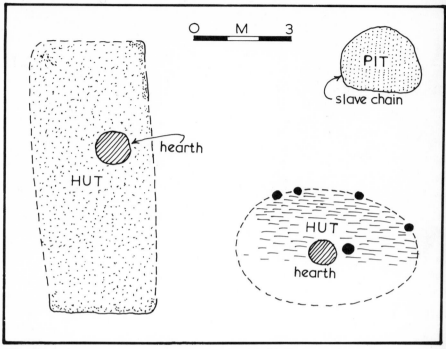

The Belgic farmstead at Park Street, Herts, c.AD.20-43.

of Italian wine. The same conclusion emerges from a study of some of the farmsteads which are to be found in the countryside around the great tribal centres. Some of these, such as Nutfield and Crookhams in Hertfordshire, seem to have been ditched oval enclosures but in most cases only the dwelling huts and nearby pits and hearths have been recorded. As in the *oppida* the huts are a mixture of circular and rectangular ones. The circular timber-frame huts from sites such as Brixworth (Northants), Shakenoak (Oxon), Park Street and Lockleys (Herts) are all small buildings of between 12 and 18 feet diameter which differ from timber huts of the preceding period mainly in having only a single circle of wall posts and no porch. In some cases, notably at Park Street and Lockleys, circular huts were succeeded by rectangular ones with chalk or clay floors. In terms of floor area these appear to be as much as half as large again as the circular huts, but they are still very simple buildings providing only limited comfort. They were, nevertheless, the homes of men of wealth. Several of these farmstead sites have produced examples of Belgic coinage and it is unlikely that this medium of exchange circulated amongst the mass of the population. Equally there are a number of very rich Belgic burials from rural locations, away from contemporary *oppida*, and it is likely that they relate to as yet undiscovered farmsteads. In one case, at Panshanger, Welwyn (Herts), a wealthy grave was uncovered only two hundred yards away from the partially explored farmstead at Grubs Barn. Finally, it is surely significant that many of these Belgic farmsteads have come to light beneath later Roman villas—the latest example is one at Gorhambury (Herts)—suggesting a link between the wealthy families who owned the villa estates of the Roman period and those who owned the Belgic farmsteads of the preceding age.

There is still remarkably little archaeological evidence of the type of economy practised on these Belgic farms in South-East England, but such as there is bears out what Caesar, Strabo and others have to say on the subject. Caesar was impressed by the number of cattle kept by the Belgic tribes in Britain, and mentions that a great number of them were found inside the *oppidum* which he captured, probably at Wheathampstead. Strabo similarly lists cattle and hides among the principal exports from Southern Britain. He also mentions corn, and the appearance of an ear of corn as an emblem on the coins of the Catuvellauni seems to emphasise its economic importance. To what extent increased corn production resulted from the introduction of a heavier plough-share, able to turn over heavier soils than had previously come under the plough, and to what extent it was brought about by improved organisation of land and labour is not certain. The Belgae certainly employed slaves on their farms, and slave chains of the period have been found at several sites. At Park Street one such chain was found in a pit near the main living hut, and close to a second, oval hut thought to be possibly the slaves' quarters. Slaves are another 'commodity' which appears in Strabo's list of British exports, and it is clear that Britain was able to maintain a thriving trade with Roman-occupied Gaul in the century before the Roman invasion of Britain itself. Apart from the cattle, hides, corn and slaves already mentioned, Strabo lists hunting dogs, gold, silver and iron as other commodities finding a ready market on the continent. Most of these exports would have been obtained within the growing boundaries of the Belgic king-

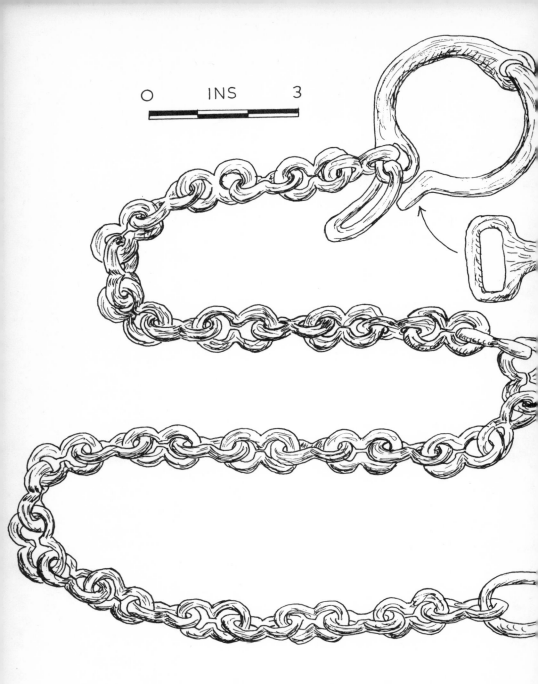

An iron slave chain from the Belgic farmstead at Park Street

Silver cups from Chieftain burials.

doms, but some such as gold and silver must have been obtained as gifts, tribute or trade-goods from much further west in Britain. Almost certainly, however, the bulk of all of these goods was traded through Camulodunum, where considerable quantities of the luxuries obtained in return have been found in excavation. Strabo mentions ivory trinkets, amber, glassware and pottery as Britain's principal imports from the Roman world, and this information is partly confirmed and partly amplified by archaeological discoveries. Glassware for example includes Gallic vessels and occasional gaming sets, and pottery includes both Gallic wares and Arretine tableware from Itlay. But we also have archaeological evidence of other imports not mentioned by Strabo—silver cups from Italy, bronze jugs, bowls and wine-strainers from Italy and Gaul, oil from Spain, and quantities of Italian wine.

By far the best evidence of the importation of these luxuries comes from a series of Belgic burials whose distribution centres on the Welwyn area (Herts). In these the body is characteristically cremated and buried with a superb display of wealth. At Panshanger the grave-goods included a set of glass gaming pieces in four colours, a bronze-bowl and strainer, a silver cup, and five wine amphorae, as well as many other items. Other graves have produced hearth furniture which once stood, presumably, in small huts like those at Park Street and elsewhere—impressive iron fire-dogs, spits and tripods. Feasting and drinking seem to have played an important part in the life of the men buried in these 'chieftain' burials, and no doubt they were waited on by the men and women whose cremated bodies, buried without any grave-goods at all, are often found in the area around one of the chieftain

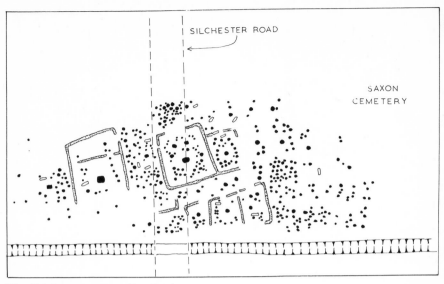

SILCHESTER ROAD

SAXON CEMETERY

The Belgic cemetery at Verulamium.

burials. The picture of a two-tier society is indeed painted by Caesar himself, and it is supported by much larger Belgic cemeteries such as that found at Verulamium. Over four hundred and fifty graves were found here, many of them scattered apparently haphazardly across the area of the cemetery. Others clustered thickly in groups, and in at least six areas there were orderly groups of graves laid out within ditched enclosures. In each of these there was a central grave with an ample supply of grave-goods including imported pottery, silver mirrors and coins. The remaining graves were poorly furnished and were arranged in a circle or square around the central one.

It may be that the social organisation to which such cemeteries attest was basically not very different from that which obtained in regions outside the area of Belgic occupation. Certainly there are signs elsewhere of an aristocracy whose wealth far outstripped that of the rest of the population. In East Anglia there are the hoards of exquisite gold and electrum torcs from Snettisham and elsewhere, and rich collections of horse-trappings. From Bulbury in Dorset there is a large deposit of metalwork including a bronze mirror, tankard, and bowls, together with a sword and scabbard, and further horse pieces. A little further west another superb bronze mirror has recently been found in

A horse-bit from the Polden Hill hoard, Soms.

a native farmstead at Holcombe (Devon). A third mirror was found in a very rich female burial at Birdlip (Glos), which also contained two bronze bowls, various bronze trinkets and a necklace of amber, jet and other stones. From Somerset there is the rich hoard of bronze horse equipment found on Polden Hill and from the South-West in general a group of decorated bronze neck-rings. In areas such as Dorset, Somerset and Gloucester these aristocracies may indeed have been of Belgic origin themselves, and certainly the tribes here issue coins of Belgic type. Political organisation apart, however, these peoples seem to have been affected very little by the arrival of the Belgae, and their lives and culture continued in much the same way as before. In Dorset and Wiltshire, for example, the major hill-forts continued in occupation, and in the last fifty years before the Roman invasion saw further additions to their defences and the densest settlement of their interiors which they ever experienced. Forts like Maiden Castle, Hambledon, and Hod Hill were occupied by dozens, even hundreds, of circular huts to which small tracks and roadways gave access. At Maiden Castle, Pilsdon Pen, and South Cadbury, structures which were probably shrines or sanctuaries have been identified, and at South Cadbury evidence of a skilled bronzesmith at work has been recovered. In terms of population, public buildings, and the presence of specialist craftsmen, these southern hill-forts seem to be moving nearer still to becoming true townships. Contemporary farmsteads show few if any changes from those which had existed in these same areas for the preceding five

A decorated neck-ring from Wraxall, Soms, lst cent. AD.

The multiple ramparts of Hambledon Hill, Dorset.

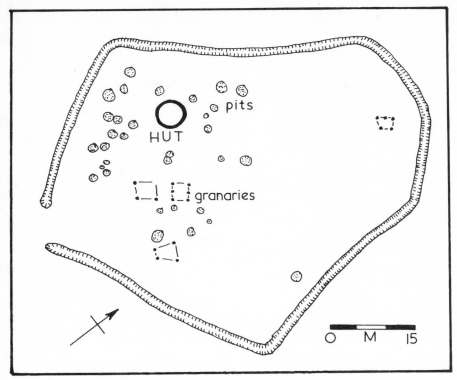

A farmstead at Tollard Royal, Wilts, c. AD. 30-40.

centuries. Storage pits, four-post granaries and round huts are still characteristic of these farms, whether they be associated with roughly circular enclosures like those at Woodcuts (Dorset) and Rotherley (Wilts), or more angular ones like that which surrounds the farmstead at Tollard Royal (Wilts). Here the pits and granaries attest to the continuing importance of grain production, but the empty half of the settlement enclosure is suggestive of arrangements for the winter corraling of a herd or flock. Similarly, droveways at Woodcuts and Rotherley indicate that animals were frequently driven through the surrounding fields and emphasise the mixed nature of the farming economy.

In the South-West peninsula the economy remained essentially pastoral, and earlier settlements such as the cliff castles and small fortified settlements with annexes, continued in occupation. In Cornwall they were probably joined from the mid-second century BC onwards by

135

new settlements characterised by an oval or circular earthwork enclosing up to two acres and containing usually two or three circular huts, as at Trevisker and Castle Gotha, built close to the earthwork for protection from the elements. In West Cornwall these 'rounds', as the enclosures are called, sometimes contain more elaborate huts known as 'courtyard houses', which consist of several small cell-like rooms used for living, sleeping, storage and working, which open off a small central yard. The 'rounds' are much more numerous than the cliff castles and small forts, and it has been suggested that they were dependants of the local chieftains who occupied the latter,

In Somerset and Gloucester much larger communities existed, some in hill-forts like Worleybury, and others in villages of which the best known, though in some respects atypical, are the so-called 'lake-villages' of Glastonbury and Meare. At the former, two phases of occupation have now been recognised, the first of which was characterised by small square houses raised up on strong oak piles. The excellent carpentry displayed in these buildings extended to a wide variety of other products which have survived the centuries in the damp conditions on the site. These included wheeled carts, horizontal looms, wooden bowls, spoons, mallets, and a host of other items. They also used 'currency bars' of iron, ingots of iron in long blades made to roughly a standard weight and used as a form of currency. Caesar mentioned these curious bars in his description of Britain, and many examples have been found in Southern and Western England. They were largely replaced, of course, by coinage proper, in the later-first century BC. By this time the Glastonbury village had completely changed in appearance as new settlers here occupied circular huts built on artifi-

Iron currency bars from Gloucestershire.

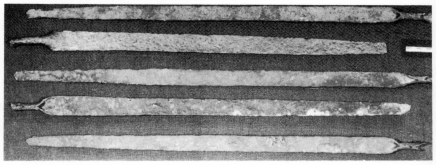

The wall galleries in the *broch* at Dun Telve, Inverness

cial platforms of wood and other material covered with clay floors. Although they were not the accomplished carpenters that their predecessors were they had wide trading connections as evidenced by their use of Cornish tin, Kimmeridge shale, Mendip lead and even Gallic glass.

Across the Severn there was much less contact with areas far afield. Throughout Wales hill-forts were still occupied, and remained so down to the Roman conquest, which was only gradually accomplished between 50 AD and 78 AD. In the South-West, however, a new settlement type may have emerged in the last two centuries BC—the so-called 'rath', a roughly circular earthwork enclosure containing the circular huts of a community of perhaps thirty people. Nearly two hundred such 'raths' are known in South-West Wales but few have been even sampled by excavation. The one completely excavated example at Walesland Rath (Pembroke) proved to have at least six circular huts, a six-post rectangular building—perhaps a granary —and timber ranges built around the perimeter, against the enclosing bank. These timber ranges recall the evidence of similar structures found inside the *duns* of the North and West of Scotland, and referred to in the previous chapter. The *duns* and *crannogs* of the West persisted until the end of the first century AD, and indeed sometimes long after, and the defended enclosures and hill-forts of the Southern Uplands and Cheviots were also occupied into the Roman period. In the North and North-West of Scotland however the *duns* gave way to, and possibly even sired, a new highly-defensible type of settlement known as a *broch*. These *brochs* were massive circular towers with battered outer wall faces, originally standing to between thirty and forty feet in height. The walls were broad, sometimes with chambers built into them at ground level and with a succession of galleries running around them at higher levels, linked by stone-built stairways. From these access could be gained to one or two wooden floors supported by rafters set onto the wall and held at the centre by a ring of posts. In other words, the *brochs* were two or three storey houses which, once the narrow doorway had been blocked, were almost completely safe from attack. The *brochs* were only replaced by less heavily defended types of house in the second century AD, by which time even the Northern Isles had come into contact with the power of Rome, and Southern Scotland had indeed been overrun by the invader.

A stone staircase in the *broch* at Dun Telve

The White Horse at Uffington, Berks.

In Southern England the Roman invasion was not unwelcome to some who saw in it a chance to free themselves from the oppression of neighbouring tribes. Initially the power struggle was between Belgic and non-Belgic peoples, but from the middle of the first century BC it became a contest between rival Belgic kingdoms. Indeed Caesar himself exploited the hostility between the neighbouring tribes of Essex and Hertforshire, the Trinovantes and the Catuvellauni respectively, during his invastion of 54 BC. The struggle between these two tribes which Caesar records was the beginning of the long rise to power of the Catuvellauni. From their centre of power in Hertfordshire, Middlesex and Buckinghamshire they gradually expanded in all directions. Under their king Tasciouvanus between about 20 BC and 5 AD. the tribe extended their frontiers into Northants, Oxford, Berkshire, Surrey and West Kent. He was followed by the greatest of all British kings — Cunobelinus (Old King Cole) — who between about 5 AD and 40AD pushed the Catuvellaunian empire to new limits. The territory of the Trinovantes was swallowed up by 7 AD, and with it the invaluable *oppidum* and harbour at Camulodunum, which Cunobelinus promptly made his own capital. To the North parts of the territory, the

140

Iceni and Coritani were absorbed, whilst to the South-East the Cantiaci of Kent were overrun.

The pressure was now mounting, westwards, on the kingdom of the Atrebates. This was a powerful tribe, whose founding dynast was Commius, at one time a Gallic ally of Caesar who rebelled against Rome and fled to Britain in about 50 BC. A succession of kings, who all claim, on their coins, to be sons of Commius maintained a sizeable kingdom in Berks, Hants and West Sussex until about 20 AD. Then a brother of Cunobelin, known as Epaticcus, began to carve out a new Catuvellaunian kingdom in the northern part of the Atrebatic one. By 25 AD the old tribal capital at Calleva (Silchester) had fallen to the invaders, and by the time Cunobelin died, almost all the Atrebatic kingdom had come under his sway. At the same time the tribe inhabiting Gloucester and Somerset, the Dobunni, had begun to retreat before the advancing Catuvellauni, aided by the internal break-up of the Dobunnic kingdom into rival factions. To what extent Rome was involved, directly or indirectly in these affairs is difficult to assess, but involved it certainly was and indeed the several references to events in Britain in the Roman authors of this period emphasise the point. Although the involvement was not, with the exception of Caesar, military, it was political. Caesar himself had laid treaty obligations on both the Catuvellauni and the Trinovantes, and from this time up until the Roman invasion of 43 AD we can identify a number of British kings who had treaty relations or other formal political contacts with Rome. The Atrebatic kings almost certainly used Roman die-cutters for their coinage, which was not only based on Roman issues but also bore the latin title Rex, a title presumably bestowed on successive kings by the Romans at a time when treaty-relationships were renewed. As it happened it was in fact precisely this treaty relationship between Rome and the Atrebates which eventually brought about the Roman invasion. When the final remnant of the Atrebatic kingdom was overrun by Cunobelinus' sons in the years immediately after his death, the deposed Atrebatic king Verica fled—like other deposed British monarchs before him—to Rome. He asked for Roman intervention and, mainly because Claudius had good reasons of his own for interfering, he got it. In 43 AD the Roman legions crossed the Channel and brought Britain into the world of written history.

SUGGESTIONS FOR FURTHER READING

It is impossible in a book of this size to give a full bibliography for the three hundred sites mentioned in the text, let alone for the many hundreds of other important sites which have had to be passed over without mention. For the student, who will want to consult the original reports on many of these sites, those books listed below which are marked with an asterisk will be found to be invaluable works of reference, in addition to the excellent texts which they incorporate. For the general reader I would recommend, first, Stuart Piggott's *Ancient Europe* (1965), a well-written and beautifully illustrated book which puts Britain firmly in its Continental perspective. Thereafter the other books listed below may be read with pleasure and benefit, and illustrated, up-to-date accounts of new excavations on prehistoric sites can be read in the frequent issues of the two journals mentioned.

BOOKS

*B.W. Cunliffe, *Iron Age Communities in Britain* (1974)
A. Fox, *South West England* (1974)
E. Hadingham, *Ancient Carvings in Britain* (1974)
*D. Harding, *The Iron Age in Lowland Britain* (1974)
Ordnance Survey, *Map of Southern Britain in the Iron Age* (1962)
*S. Piggott, *The Neolithic Cultures of the British Isles* (1954)
*C. Renfrew (ed), *Britain Prehistory. A New Outline* (1974)
A.L.F. Rivet (ed), *The Iron Age in Northern Britain* (1966)
D. Simpson (ed), *Economy and Settlement in Neolithic and Early Bronze Age Britain and Europe* (1971)

JOURNALS

Current Archaeology (6 issues a year)
Antiquity (4 issues a year)

INDEX

KILPHEDIR

MIGDALE

CLAVA

CORRIEMONY

DUN TELVE

FINAVON

DALGETY

TRAPAIN LAW

BRAIDWOOD

EILDON

YEAVERING

HUCKHOE

BURNSWARK

W. BRANDON

HEATHERY BURN

BALLNAGILLY